Architecture of a Activation Function Layer Employing Composite Charge Reuse Methodology for Tech-Enabled Settings

Míng Yǒu

Architecture of a Activation Function Layer Employing Composite Charge Reuse Methodology for Tech-Enabled Settings

First Edition June 2025

Written by Míng Yǒu

TABLE OF CONTENTS

CHAPTER NO.	TITLE	PAGE NO.

CHAPTER 1

INTRODUCTION

1.1 INTRODUCTION

Very Large Scale Integration (VLSI) involved in the Integrated Circuit (IC) formation by merging millions of Metal Oxide Semiconductor (MOS) transistors in a single chip. These ICs are preferred in most of the security applications due to its physical and electrical properties. In this modern digital world, security plays an important role to protect the personal information from the hackers. Since security is one of the emerging fields, various kind of security issues are analyzed and different kinds of security approaches are presented by the researchers to mitigate these issues. The researchers not only focused the security, they also focused an optimized design. The design should occupy less area, low power consumption and it should achieve high performance. However, in the VLSI field, considerations like area, power, and latency are traded off.

The design of digital circuits is a challenging and tedious task because it consumes more power due to the utilization of functional integration blocks, clock speed, geometrical process, etc. The scaling process employed in the design enhanced the number of transistors as well as operation of the chip. But the scaling process can attain high speed leads to high performance of the overall design. The voltage scaling process reduced the threshold voltage but gradually increased the leakage current. Nowadays, the leakage power is also one of the major issues presented in the VLSI circuit designs. As per the report from International Roadmap Semiconductor (ITRS), the dissipation of leakage power has impact on the overall power consumption of the device (Kaedi*et al.* 2019). There are different approaches are presented in the technology level and circuit level to reduce the leakage power and dynamic power.

1.2 OBJECTIVES OF VLSI CIRCUIT DESIGN

The three major factors behind the design of each and every VLSI circuit are listed as follows

- Area
- Power
- Delay

For an effective VLSI circuit design, the design should be portable, it should consume less power and is should be operated with high speed.

1.3 COMPLEMENTARY MOS (CMOS) TECHNOLOGY

CMOS technology is constructed using n type and p type Metal Oxide Semiconductor Field Effect Transistors (MOSFET). It is one of the technologies equipped for forming Ics, memory chips, controllers, processors, etc. MOSFET was first introduced in 1959 at Bell laboratory, and then NMOS and PMOS are developed in 1960. Both the NMOS and PMOS are combined and CMOS is formed in 1963. This technology is applicable for the design of analog circuits, digital circuits and mixed signal circuits.

In the 1970s, CMOS technology was only employed in a few consumer markets, such as electronic watches. In the 1980s, however, VLSI technology shifted to CMOS because of benefits such as low power, high noise margin, wider temperature and voltage operation range, overall circuit simplicity, electro migration problem, dependability, and layout flexibility.

In the 1980s, the advent of VLSI accelerated the integration density of a single chip to millions of transistors. For VLSI digital and mixed-signal designs, CMOS is now the most used technology. CMOS logic is faster, more adaptable to low supply voltage, and uses low power consumption than Transistor-Transistor Logic (TTL).

Two important parameters of CMOS technology based devices are noise immunity and leakage power. In this technology, the source of PMOS transistors is connected to supply voltage (V_{dd}) and the source of NMOS transistor is connected to ground. It can support for performing multiple logic functions in a single chip. When compared with the existing logic families, the power dissipated by CMOS technology is less. The power consumed by CMOS logic is also 7 times lesser than the power consumed by NMOs logic and 1,00,000 times lesser than transistor- transistor logic (TTL). So it is the most common technology preferred in the VLSI circuit designs.

MOSFETs, in the form of complementary MOS (CMOS) circuits, are widely used in digital circuits. With n- and p-channel MOSFETs coupled together on the same chip, CMOS technology fabricates NMOS and PMOS transistors. It is the most widely used digital integrated circuits technique, with several benefits over employing NMOS and PMOS transistors independently. The fundamental motivation for creating complementary MOSFETs (CMOS) technology was to achieve high speed and low power dissipation in logic gates for digital circuits.

For L-band personal communications, a monolithic microwave integrated circuit (MMIC) with an internally matched, extremely low operation voltage amplifier has been constructed in a 0.35-m silicon-oninsulator (SOI) complementary metal oxide semiconductor (CMOS) technology. With a drain voltage of 0.6 V and a current of 2 mA, the MMIC amplifier has a gain of 6.4 dB and a noise figure of 4.8 dB at 1.6 GHz. The Gain/Power quotient of the MMIC amplifier is 5.33 dB/mW, which is the highest ever reported for Si CMOS MMIC technology.

CMOS allows for the creation of a wide range of powerful analogue and digital circuit topologies. CMOS logic devices are similar to BJT logic devices in that they are switched by voltage rather than current; no current flows into the CMOS gate. CMOS technology is preferred to design multiple logic gates and digital circuits. The PMOS transistors used in this technology can generate low resistance between the source and drain terminals and NMOS transistors can generate high resistance between the source and drain terminals. In this technology the gate of both the NMOS and PMOS transistors are connected, similarly the drain of both the NMOS and PMOS transistors are connected leads to the current reduction. The NMOS in this technology conducts during high supply voltage and the PMOS in this technology conducts during low supply voltage. Because of this conduction property it can reduce the power consumption as well as heat generation.

1.4 POWER CONSUMPTION IN CMOS TECHNOLOGY

In this modern digital world, the technology development placed a significant role in the life of human beings and so semiconductor industries focused this as their major aim. To attain this, the high performance as well as handy electronic devices is focused. This can be achieved by the varying the size of MOS transistors. The variations occurred in the MOS transistors leads to the fruitfulness in wiring densities as well as packing process. The resizing process carried out in the Ics generates high complexity and the time need to complete the whole computation also very high. To mitigate these issues, in the past researches the researchers reuse the circuit designs and Intellectual

Property (IP) is considered for generating logical circuit designs (Vijaya Chandra Kurapati, 2006). This IP is preferred by the circuit designers because, it consumes less computation time to complete the circuit design.

Jazz Semiconductor's 0.18-mum improved RF CMOS process was used to develop and build an ultra-wideband CMOS integrated sampling mixer subsystem. To achieve high gain, quick sampling, low noise figure, low power consumption, and improved RF power efficiency, a two-stage switching method is used to simultaneously combine a Low-Noise Amplifier (LNA) with a sampler. Two synchronized strobes generated on-chip switch the LNA and sample-and-hold capacitor. The sampling strobe's characteristics, as well as the sampling clock jitter's impacts on the sampling bandwidth, are described. Results demonstrate 9-12 dB voltage conversion gain, 16-25 dB noise figure, and power consumption of just 21.6 mW (with buffer) and 11.7 mW (without buffer) across dc to 3.5 GHz with a 100-MHz sampling frequency.

The implementation of circuit designs in deep submicron technology is one of the challenging and tedious tasks to the circuit designers. During these implementations, the focus of the circuit designers is to design the circuits with less power consumption. The power dissipated from the circuits designs are categorized into static power or leakage power and dynamic power. The leakage power at various CMOS technologies is compared with the dynamic power at various CMOS technologies and it is shown in Figure 1.1.

As shown in Figure 1.1, as the size of the technology is lowered, the leakage power and dynamic power consumption increases. The technology size is indirectly proportional to the leakage power consumption and dynamic power consumption. The advancement in technology leads to the improvement in power consumption as well as power density. The effect of this process also happened in cooling, packing and reliability.

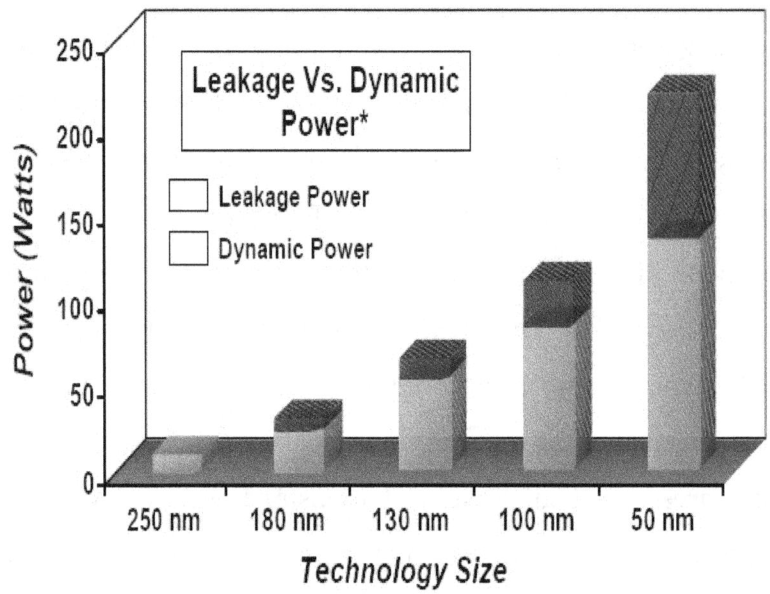

Figure 1.1 Comparison of leakage and dynamic power in various CMOS Technologies

Analytically, adiabatic and conventional CMOS NAND/NOR gates are evaluated at the gate level vs. fan-in. The comparison was done using an assigned power source that was set to consume the minimum amount of power consumption. The research resulted in simple equations that are independent of the technology utilized and allow us to see how the power advantage of adiabatic logic decreases as the complexity of the implemented Boolean function grows. Spice simulations employing 0.8- and 0.35-/spl mu/m CMOS technology supported the analytical results. The research demonstrates that for frequencies less than roughly 30 MHz, the adiabatic style is favorable with the technologies chosen for the non-optimized design.

It is suggested to create a scalable low-power high-voltage driver using just ordinary low-voltage CMOS transistors. A stacked MOSFET high-voltage driver is used in this circuit. Low power consumption (in the microwatts), compact size, scalability, and self-sufficiency distinguish the suggested design. The primary disadvantages to be considered are its slow switching speed (microseconds) and the fact that it can only be used with capacitive and high resistive loads. The simulation findings achieved through the execution of different designs in 0.18 um CMOS technology is presented in this research.

Power consumption is one of the major factors used for making the reliable design. The devices which are consumed less power making the devices more reliable (Texas Instruments, 1997). The power consumed by the devices can be categorized into two different types.

- Dynamic power consumption
- Static power consumption

1.4.1 Static Power Consumption

Static power consumption is computed based on leakage current and so it is termed as leakage power. It is measured during the idle state of the transistors. The leakage power of the device is indirectly proportional to the process technology. The leakage power can be computed by the following expression

$$\text{Leakage power } P_{leakage} = \sum \text{cell leakage} \quad (1.1)$$

The leakage current of the diode presented in the CMOS devices can be computed by the following mathematical expression

$$\text{Leakage current } I_{leakage} = i_{rs}\,(e^{\frac{qV}{kT}} - 1) \quad (1.2)$$

Here i_{rs} = reverse saturation current

q = charge of electron (1.602 x 10^{-19} C)

V = voltage of the diode

k = Boltzmann's constant (1.38 x 10^{-23} J/K)

T = temperature

Static power consumption can be computed by multiplying the leakage current of the device with the supply voltage of the device. The static power consumption can be computed by the following mathematical expression

$$\text{Static power } P_{static} = \sum I_{leakage} \times \text{Supply Voltage} \tag{1.3}$$

The static power consumption of the CMOS device can be reduced by either reducing the leakage current or supply voltage. If both the parameters are low, the static power consumed by the CMOS device is also less.

1.4.2 Dynamic Power Consumption

Dynamic power consumption can be computed based on the switching activity of the transistors and so it is also called as switching power. The dynamic power consumption of the device is indirectly proportional to the process technology. The dynamic power consumption of the CMOS device is the summation of transient power consumption and capacitive load power consumption. The dynamic power consumption can be computed by the following mathematical expression

$$\text{Dynamic power } P_{dynamic} = P_{transient} + P_{capacitive} \tag{1.4}$$

Here $P_{transient}$ denotes the transient power consumption and $P_{capacitive}$ denotes capacitive load power consumption.

Transient power consumption is occurred because of the flow of current in the CMOS devices during the transition of the transistors state from one to other. The current may be switching current or the current flow from supply to the ground. Transient power consumption can be computed by the following mathematical expression

$$P_{transient} = V_{cc}^2 \times C_{pd} \times f_i \times N_{sw} \quad (1.5)$$

Here V_{cc} = Supply voltage

C_{pd} = Capacitance power dissipation

f_i = frequency of input signal

N_{sw} = Number of bits switched

The C_{pd} of CMOS device can be computed by computing the operating current without connecting the load capacitance.

The capacitive load power consumption can be computed when the same load is connected with all the outputs and when these are operated with same frequency. The capacitive load power consumption can be computed by the following mathematical expression

$$P_{capacitive} = V_{cc}^2 \times C_L \times f_o \times N_{sw} \quad (1.6)$$

Here C_L = Load capacitance

f_o = Output signal frequency

If the output is connected with the multiple loads and operated at different frequencies, then capacitive load power consumption can be computed by the following mathematical expression

$$P_{capacitive} = \sum(C_{Lm} \times F_{om}) \times V_{cc}^2 \tag{1.7}$$

Here C_{Lm}= Load capacitance connected to multiple outputs

F_{om}= Multiple outputs operating at multiple frequencies

1.5 POWER DISSIPATION IN CMOS

The advanced handy portable electronic devices require high density Integrated Circuits (Ics) with low power consumption. As the size of the transistors is reduced over the years in the VLSI technology, the reduction process in the power dissipation is complicated task. The power dissipation in CMOS circuits can be categorized as follows

- Static power dissipation (S_{pd})
- Dynamic power dissipation (D_{pd})
- Short circuit power dissipation (SC_{pd})

The total power dissipation in CMOS devices can be computed by adding static power dissipation, dynamic power dissipation and short circuit power dissipation.

$$\text{Total power dissipation } (T_{pd}) = S_{pd} + D_{pd} + SC_{pd} \tag{1.8}$$

Static power dissipation is occurred during the idle state of CMOS circuits. In this state, the transistors are in the OFF position generate some leakage current leads to power dissipation. The diode equation is preferred to describe the leakage current generated in CMOS circuits.

Deep-nano technologies' higher leakage power, on the one hand, and exponential rise in the number of transistors in a given die, especially in Field-Programmable Gate Arrays (FPGAs), has resulted in an increased rate of static power dissipation and power density. The breakdown of Dennard scaling has been caused by the ever-increasing static power consumption, which acts as a power wall to further transistor integration. Designers are compelled to limit the active proportion of the chip by powering down a chosen fraction of dark silicon, known to as Silicon die, to fulfill the available power budget and avoid reliability difficulties associated with excessive power density. Several interesting topologies for improving static power and energy efficiency in FPGAs have been developed.

The switching of low voltage input to high voltage input or high voltage input to low voltage input permits the MOS transistors to ON for a certain period. The current pulse generated between supply voltages to ground generates dissipation due to charging and discharging process. During charging process, the energy is dissipated in the form of heat from the power supply. During discharging process, the amount of energy stored in the capacitor placed in the output side is dissipated in the form of heat.

A unique FPGA routing switch design that employs dual-vdd technology to identify routing materials with excessive power consumption. The suggested routing switch structure requires just slight modifications to a traditional switch and can operate in three modes: sleep, low-speed, and high-speed, each with its own set of power and performance tradeoffs. Performance is compromised in low-power settings to save power consumption. To support dual-Vdd approach, this architecture uses a single supply voltage rail and the other (than conventional) voltage level is created internally by adding configuration SRAM cells and additional transistors. Indeed, this architecture takes use of non – critical paths available time slack in designs to slow down and power down the relevant routing switches.

If the rise time and fall time of the circuit has finite value, then the NMOS and PMOS transistors conducts for a certain period of time and form a track between supply voltage and ground leads to short circuit current. The process of multiplying the supply voltage with the short circuit current generates short circuit power dissipation.

Static and dynamic power is the primary sources of power in Complementary Metal-Oxide-Semiconductor (CMOS) circuits. Leakage currents, which are present in any active circuit regardless of clock rates or use situations, create static power consumption, or leakage power. The type of transistors used and the manufacturing method used determine the static power. The decrease of static power necessitates changes in low-level system design, which is outside the scope of this chapter.

1.6 POWER CONSUMPTION REDUCTION APPROACHES

Circuit designers considered different power reduction approaches to reduce the power consumed by the components of the devices. They need to compromise any of the performance such as cost, reliability, area, delay, etc to achieve low power consumption. Some of the power reduction approaches are listed as follows

- Clock Gating
- Variable frequency
- Power Gating
- Multi-threshold voltage

- Multi V_{DD} technique
- Dynamic voltage and frequency scaling

Clock Gating

Clock gating method is used for reducing the dynamic power consumption which can be computed by adding transient power consumption and capacitive load power consumption. This method can reduce the transient current by using the AND gate or NOR gate to gate the clock. This gating process reduced the dynamic current by gating the components which are not in use.

Clock gating saves power by pruning the clock tree, but it comes at the expense of adding extra logic to the circuit. Pruning the clock disables parts of the circuitry, preventing the flip-flops from switching states. Power is consumed when states are switched. When the switch is not in use, the switching power consumption drops to zero and leaving just leakage currents.

Clock gating works by using the enable criteria associated with registers to gate the clocks. To use and benefit from clock gating, a design must have these enable requirements. Because it eliminates a huge number of muxes and substitutes them with clock gating logic, this clock gating technique can save considerable die area and power. "Integrated Clock Gating" (ICG) cells are commonly used to provide clock gating logic. The clock gating logic, on the other hand, will affect the clock tree structure since it will be located within the clock tree.

Variable frequency

To obtain a desired performance, there is no need of high frequency for all the components of the devices. Every component requires specific frequency to perform better. Some components require high frequency to perform better and some components require low frequency to perform better. Hence the utilization of variable frequency in the CMOS devices reduces the dynamic power consumption.

Power Gating

Power gating methods reduce the power consumption by blocking the components which are not in use. This method reduces the leakage power consumption as well as dynamic power consumption. Externally switched power supplies are the most basic kind of power gating for reducing leakage power over time. Internal power gating can be used to turn off the block for a short duration. Power gating controllers regulate the CMOS switches that provide power to the circuitry. The power gated block's output discharges slowly. As a result, output voltage levels spend more time near the threshold voltage. This might result in a higher short circuit current.

Multi threshold voltage

The characteristics of the CMOS devices are differed by the threshold voltage of the transistors. If the gate voltage is less than threshold voltage, then the current flow between source terminal and drain terminal is termed as sub threshold current. It can be reduced by increasing the threshold voltage leads to low power consumption.

Multi V_{DD} technique

The dynamic power consumption is directly proportional to the supply voltage. So, the reduction in the supply voltage leads to the reduction in the dynamic power consumption.

Dynamic voltage and frequency scaling

Dynamic voltage scaling is used for offering the required voltages to the CMOS devices lead to the reduction in dynamic power consumption. Dynamic frequency scaling is used for delivering the specific frequency to the CMOS devices. It leads to the reduction in the dynamic power consumption as well as leakage power consumption. Because the frequency at which a chip can run is connected to the operating voltage, dynamic voltage scaling is frequently used in conjunction with frequency scaling.

Because the efficiency of some electrical components, such as voltage regulators, declines when temperature rises, power consumption may rise as well. Increases in voltage or frequency may raise system power needs even more than the CMOS formula predicts, and vice versa, because increased power usage may increase temperature.

Dynamic frequency scaling is rarely a good solution to save switching power on its own. Because of the V2 component and the fact that current CPUs are heavily designed for low power idle states, saving the most amount of power idle state. Dynamic voltage scaling is also required. In most constant-voltage scenarios, it is more economical to operate at peak speed for a short period and then stay in a deep idle state for longer than it is to run at a reduced clock rate for a long time and then just stay in a light idle state for a short time. Reduced voltage and clock rate, on the other hand, can alter such trade-offs.

1.7 ENERGY EFFICIENCY IN DIGITAL CIRCUITS

Due to the rapid improvement in handy and portable electronic devices, energy efficiency is the major concern of the circuit designers, because it is preferred in most of the real time applications in the modern digital world. These handy devices are designed with battery which needs to have long life capacity and it needs to consume low power. These are also designed with high reliability and high performance. Different researches are carried out by the researchers, to reduce the power consumption and they give multiple solutions to reduce the power consumption of the devices. Some of these techniques used in MOSFET based devices are variation in threshold voltage and variation in supply voltage. The researchers also provide the power reduction approaches in the different categorization of abstraction levels such as circuit level, device level and system level. But the major issues in VLSI circuits are the tradeoff between area, delay and power. So, the designers need to focus these factors to make an optimized design.

The variation in the supply voltage is used in the VLSI based devices to make the design with power efficient. The variation in the supply voltage without the variation in threshold voltage affects the overall performance of the devices. So there is a need of proper proportionality between the two factors named supply voltage and threshold voltage to design high performance devices. But, in some specific cases, the leakage current is increased by reducing the threshold voltage. To mitigate these limitations, different kinds of approaches are presented by the researchers to create an optimized circuit design which is well suited for real time applications.

The energy consumption of the devices can be computed by computing the product of power consumption and time required t complete the process. The energy efficiency of the device is depending on the power consumption and time. Hence, for an optimized circuit design, the major parameter needs to focus is less power consumption. The power consumption of the device is directly proportional to the area occupation of the device or utilization of number of logic gates. The improvement in the resource utilization tends to the improvement in the power consumption which is the major reason for high energy consumption. So, the significant parameter needs to focus in most of the devices are power consumption.

1.8 HIGH SECURITY IN DIGITAL CIRCUITS

Humans' everyday routines in the modern scenario are entirely dependent on digital technology. The personal details of human beings are stored digitally for multiple purposes and so it should be secured and protected from fraudulent activities. Due to the technology advancement, there is also a possibility for hacking the data during data transmission. The researchers also introduced multiple security approaches to prevent the data hacking.

High security in Internet of Things (IoT) can be achieved through cryptography where the data is transmitted via wireless channel. The Internet of Things (IoT) is a networked system that can be used for infrastructure, industrial, commercial, and consumer applications, as well as monitoring, automation, and communication. It is made up of interconnected things, devices, electrical machines, digital machines, electronic appliances, humans, and animals, each with a unique identity allowing data flow between networks. It does not necessitate human-to-computer or human-to-human interaction. With the use of smart devices like Bluetooth, Zigbee, and sensors, it can send data to the network (Upadhyay *et al.* 2019). Figure 1.2 shows how the internet connects a variety of items of various sizes and computations to build IoT. It is also known as the Internet of Everything; however it has several drawbacks, such as high power consumption, complexity, and processing time (Dhananjay Singh *et al.* 2015). Network security is a fundamental concern in the practical application of IoT devices. Because high-security ciphers employ a large number of logic gates, they consume a lot of power (Abhijit Patil *et al.* 2015).

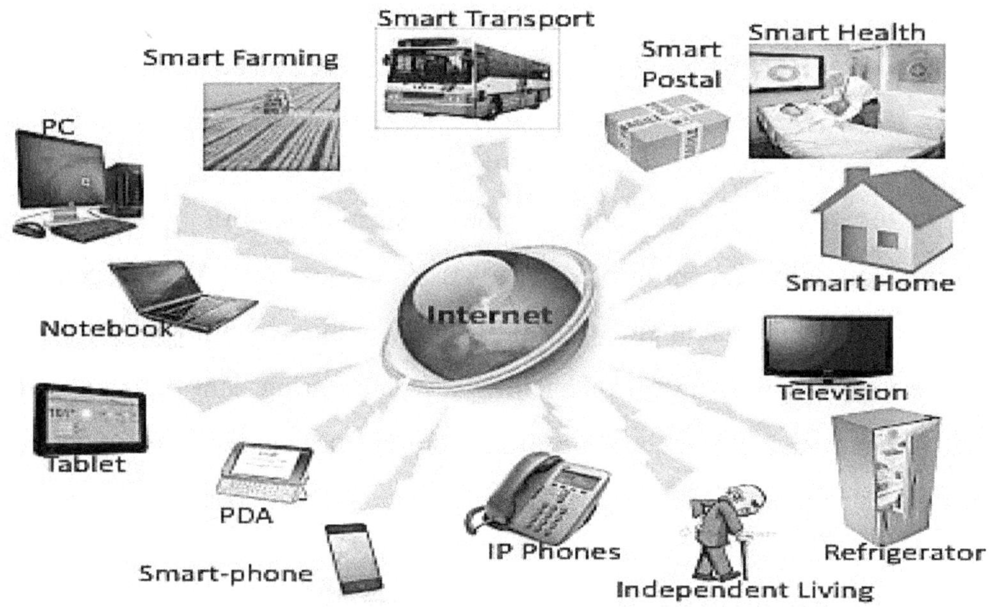

Figure 1.2 IoT Network

The cryptography can be categorized into

- Symmetric cryptography
- Asymmetric cryptography

In symmetric key cryptography, same key is used for both encryption and decryption process whereas in asymmetric cryptography, different keys are used for encryption and decryption process. Advanced Encryption Standard (AES) enhanced the security due to its computation process such as sub bytes, shift rows, mix columns and add round key (Muthavhine & Sumbwanyambe 2018).

The amount of data transmitted has no impact on the final result. When sending data, the much more significant aspect is that how secure the channel is. Cryptography is an example of a method that allows for safe data transport while maintaining secrecy and integrity. Cryptography is divided into two forms based on key distribution: symmetric key cryptography and asymmetric key cryptography. The classic algorithms for symmetric and asymmetric key cryptography as well as the proposed algorithms based on their benefits and drawbacks are considered. The relative relevance of these two cryptographic approaches are weighed. The presented algorithms proven to be extremely efficient in their respective fields, although there are several aspects that have yet to be properly studied in relation to these algorithms.

The Internet of Things (IoT) allows computing and sensing communication between devices with one another through the Internet, allowing them to exchange and receive data. Smart Home to Wearable Devices is just a few of the IoT applications. Because of the important and sensitive nature of the information shared between devices, an IoT system requires high security requirements. To secure communication between devices in an IoT system, a design combining asymmetric and symmetric cryptography is defined in this work. In comparison to utilizing an Asymmetric cryptographic technique alone, combining Symmetric and Asymmetric cryptography reduces encryption time. The use of random keys for symmetric encryption overcomes the problem of session-key distribution and enhances the symmetric encryption strategy.

1.9 ADIABATIC LOGIC

Adiabatic logic is one of the techniques used to reduce the power consumed by the devices. It is well suited for the devices which are operating around 13.56 MHz (Tessier*et al.* 2005). In adiabatic logic based circuits, the energy dissipated is approximately zero when the switching time is reduced. Due to the slower variation of power clock, there is a reduction in the energy dissipation and it also eliminates the changes in the current by maintaining the charging and discharging process as constant. The major concept behind this adiabatic logic is that reduction in the energy dissipation leads to the improvement in the switching time (Kollar 1992; Athas 1994; John S Denker 1994; Amirante 2001).

Traditional method to lowering dynamic power includes lowering supply voltage, lowering physical capacitance, and lowering switching activity. However, the majority of research has concentrated on developing adiabatic logic, which is a potential low-power solution. It is worked with the concept of switching activities which reduces the power by giving stored energy back to the supply. As a result, in low-power VLSI circuits that incorporate reversible logic, the phrase adiabatic logic is utilized. The primary design improvements are concentrated in the power clock, which is critical to the operation concept. Each phase of the power clock allows the user to achieve the adiabatic circuit design's two fundamental design principles.

If certain input criteria are met, the recovery phase of the power clock will return energy to the power clock in all four phases, resulting in significant energy savings. Nonetheless, significant intricacies in adiabatic logic design persist. Circuit implementation for time-varying power sources must be done, and computational implementation by low overhead circuit architectures must be followed, to name two such complications. Energy recovery circuits have two major challenges: first, they are sluggish by today's standards; second, they need 50% more space than normal CMOS, making even basic circuit designs more difficult.

The word adiabatic comes from thermodynamics field where the heat interchange is not carried with the environment (Kapil Mangla & Neha Mangla, 2014). The most significant advantage of adiabatic logic is that it has the capacity to restore back the stored energy during the discharging process. This process can be carried out with the assist of power clock generator which may be inductor based circuit (Athas 1994; Maksimoviu 1997) or stepwise circuit (Svensson1994; Himadri Singh, 2016).

Adiabatic logic technique is mostly preferred in ultra-low power based circuits. This technique reduced the utilization of energy by recovering the stored energy in the capacitor. It is stored as magnetic energy in inductors and charge in capacitors. The energy stored is recovered and reused for further process to reduce the energy consumption of the devices (Zachary Kahleifeh & Himanshu Thapliyal, 2021). The energy dissipated from adiabatic circuits can be computed by the following mathematical expression

$$\text{Energy dissipation} = \frac{RC}{T} CV_{dd}^{2} \tag{1.9}$$

Here,

T is capacitor's charging time

C is load capacitor

V_{dd} is supply voltage

If the charging period is greater than 2RC, then the dissipated energy of adiabatic logic based circuits is lesser than CMOS based circuits.

1.10 POWER GATING

Power gating is a technique for reducing the total leakage power of a chip by briefly turning off circuit blocks that are not in use. This brief period of shutdown is also known as "low power mode" or "inactive mode." When circuit blocks are once again required for functioning, they are switched to "active mode." These two modes are switched at the correct time and in the appropriate order to optimize power output while minimizing performance. The purpose of power gating is to reduce leakage power by turning off power to specific blocks that aren't needed in that mode. Some of the power gating techniques is listed as follows

- Sleep transistor power gating
- Stacking power gating
- Sleepy stack approach
- LECTOR approach

When compared to clock gating, power gating has a greater impact on design architecture. It lengthens time delays since power gated modes must be entered and left securely. The degree of leakage power savings attainable in such a low-power mode, as well as the energy dissipation required to enter and exit such a mode, create architectural trade-offs. Software or hardware can be used to shutting down the blocks from running. The power down actions can be scheduled using driver software. Hardware timers are an option. The alternative option is to use a specialized power management controller.

Low-leakage PMOS transistors are used as header switches in power gating to turn off power supply to components of a design that are in standby or sleep mode. Sleep transistors may be made using NMOS footer switches. The sleep transistors divide the chip's power network into two parts: a permanent power network that is connected to the power source and a virtual power network that drives the cells but can be switched off.

1.11 MOTIVATION OF THE RESEARCH WORK

Due to the advanced growth of technologies, low power consumption and low power dissipation are required in portable electronic devices. Different kinds of power dissipation techniques are introduced by the designers at various levels such as abstraction level, architectural level, system level, etc, to make the design well suited for real time applications. In addition to that the number of transistors usage in the chip is increased day by day leads to more switching process. Due to these switching activities, the power dissipation is automatically arises. To mitigate this, different solutions are presented by the researchers.

Adiabatic logic is preferred in this research work to reduce the power dissipation by reusing the energy stored in the load capacitor at each clock cycle. For reducing the power consumption, power gating approach is used. Both these techniques are used in the design of S-Box to attain high security with low power dissipation and high energy efficiency.

1.12 OBJECTIVES OF THE RESEARCH WORK

The objectives of the research work are as follows

- To design an area efficient Hybrid Energy Recovery Logic (HERL) based XOR gate by combining two different adiabatic logic techniques as ECRL and PFAL.
- To design energy efficient Gated Hybrid Energy Recovery Logic (GHERL) based XOR gate by combining HERL and power gating technique.

- Design of S-Box using HERL based XOR gate to achieve low power consumption with less area.
- Design of S-Box using GHERL based XOR gate to achieve high speed and low energy consumption.

1.13 THESIS ORGANIZATION

The organization of the thesis are stated as follows

- Chapter 1 gives an outline of power consumption, power consumption reduction strategies, and the necessity for energy-efficient and high-security devices.
- Chapter 2 briefly explains the works related with adiabatic logic, power gating and S-Box design. It also describes the merits and demerits of these approaches.
- Chapter 3 deals with the design of an area efficient Hybrid Energy Recovery Logic (HERL) based XOR gate, its logical design, simulation results and performance evaluation.
- Chapter 4 deals with the design of energy efficient Gated Hybrid Energy Recovery Logic (GHERL) based XOR gate, its logical design, simulation results and performance evaluation.
- Chapter 5 describes the S-Box design using HERL and GHERL based XOR gate. The simulation results and performance evaluation of the S-Box designs are also discussed in this chapter.

CHAPTER 2

LITERATURE SURVEY

2.1 DPA ATTACK:

Ganesh Khedkar *et al.* (2015) DPA assaults are let down by utilizing inverse RRAM modules to obfuscate the power profile. When the inverse memory is accessed in tandem with the memory module using a peripheral balancing logic block, the state memory transaction power traces are balanced. In CMOS technology, a base RTL architecture for the 128-bit AES crypto processor is devised and implemented. This baseline design is compared to balancing using RRAM and CMOS memory modules. Using the Synopsys and Cadence tool suites, as well as a Hamming weight DPA attack module written in Python, a unique simulation framework is created for obtaining the power traces. The fundamental architectures were successfully attacked, and the whole key was obtained. DPA attacks just on AES crypto processor based on inverse CMOS and RRAM were ineffective, with no keys retrieved, indicating the robustness of the proposed architecture against DPA attacks. More crucially, its RRAM balancing logic block requires one magnitude less power than pure CMOS implementation.

Kaedi *et al.* (2019), to accomplish a successful DPA attack; a non-true dynamically random power is used as a flaw of the IOA protective measure in the proposed technique. A chosen-plaintext approach is indeed the attack technique. The input data pattern is set to just be consistent inside this attack to fix a D3C countermeasure's delay. As a consequence, the countermeasure is defeated, and the DPA attack on the S-box (the S-box) introduced by IOA is efficient. All of the bits of the S-box, which was stated to be attack-proof by the D3C approach, are recovered bitwise by this assault. To begin, the S-box is modeled in a SPICE simulator to carry out the proposed concept. After that, HDL experimental results support attack on the IOA countermeasure. A Sakura-GW evaluation board as well as a Xilinx FPGA Spartan-6LX75 test-bed is used in the experiment.

Kazuyuki Tanimura & Nikil D Dutt (2012), Differential power analysis (DPA) attacks find a association between power consumption and secret data in crypto-hardware. The homogeneous dual-rail logic (HDRL) proposed in just this paper is a standard cell DPA assault countermeasure that potentially ensures perfectly balanced power consumption and considerably increases DPA attack resistance. HDRL reliably avoids DPA attacks in all situations, as per our experiments on the AES S-Box circuit.

Yu Weize & SelçukKöse (2016) the theoretical basis of deploying various on-chip voltage converters as a countermeasure against Differential Power Analysis (DPA) attacks is analyzed. An in-depth mathematical analysis of a recognizing Converter-Reshuffling (CoRe) technique is described, with measurement to disclose (MTD) being utilized to evaluate a reliability of the proposed on-chip CoRe regulator to that of conventional on-chip voltage regulators. It is proposed to use the CoRe approach to implement a DPA-resistant and lightweight Appropriate Encryption Standard (AES) engine. The effect of voltage regulator location both centralized and spread, on the privacy of a pipelined AES engine is investigated. The link here between clock frequency of the device under attack and the voltage regulator's switching frequency is explored for security implications. The suggested enhanced pipelined AES engine with a centralized on-chip CoRe regulator has an MTD value of over 9100 times that of an unsecured AES engine.

Wang *et al.* (2018) in this study, ridge analysis is used to address the power variability problem that DPA assaults have. It has been shown that these innovative methods outperform state-of-the-art methods and are more generically applicable to nano scale chips through both theory and experiments.

Arunmani (2019), this paper, introduce the Secure Double Rate Register (SDRRs) as a Register Transfer Level (RTL) countermeasures standard (AES)-128 designs are utilized in the SDRR to strengthen the security of crypto-systems against PAAs. By computing a computational path, the production of random and actual information is secured to protect both combinational and sequential logics. To produce random information, the prior RTL prevention approach necessitates the use of a fake combinational route. This study describes a novel design process for implementing a protected DPA resistant crypto-system. An analytical result reveals that the power consumption variations can be reduced for the longest duration possible.

Dhanesh (2017) this paper presents to circumvent DPA attacks in smart cards, a new logic called body Biased Adiabatic Dynamic Differential logic (BADDL) was developed. For forward body biasing, a voltage of 0.25V is used. For this logic, all logical operations use a consistent amount of power, preventing the attacker from identifying the logical operation and therefore preventing the secret key from being disclosed. When comparing the average power of BADDL to another ADDL logic called Performance adiabatic dynamic differential logic (PADDL) and CMOS logic, the benefits of this logic become clear. At 45nm Technology, this is achieved in Cadence Virtuoso.

Yuyu Zhang *et al.* (2011), in this paper, a new multi-level design strategy for protecting encryption algorithms from the DPA attack DPA-resistant techniques is often separated into two categories: software and hardware. Hardware-based solutions contradict DPA at a lower level and ensure higher countermeasure performance, whereas software-based methods are substantially cost – effective. The techniques of WDDL and dynamic cryptosystem are integrated, and present a complete DPA countermeasure on both the algorithmic and logic levels, considering both expense and reliability into account. The dynamic cryptosystem significantly improves attack difficulty, while WDDL is used to balance power consumption leaks. DPA attacks can therefore be efficiently countered at a reasonable cost.

Miao Yuan (2015), to enhance its efficiency, an optimal technique is provided. The success rate of this technique is twice as high as that of the standard absolute difference and sum merging functions, as per simulation data depending on multiple combining features. Physical traces acquired on an FPGA device data backup the concept.

Kazuyuki Tanimura (2010), This research presents ExCCel, a computational annealing-based approach for generating and exploring complementary cell combinations in order to reduce the power consumption reliance and overheads associated with conventional cells. The AES S-Box circuit with these investigated additional cells requires 6.1 percent and 2.1 percent more space and energy, respectively, than WDDL, which requires 100.3 percent and 93.4 percent. In many circumstances, ExCCeL improves WDDL in terms of DPA attack resistance.

Girish B Ratanpal *et al.* (2004), the paper describes a circuit that may be used to prevent information leaking across the power supply pin side channel. The suppression circuit’s design, simulation results, and limitations are discussed. This countermeasure increases the number of power trace samples needed to carry out a DPA assault substantially is shown. The countermeasure does not necessitate any assumptions about the device in protection's design.

Daheng Vue *et al.* (2009), a unique Look-Up-Table (LUT) Based Differential Logic (LBDL) is introduced in this research. Power consumption of LBDL gates is constant despite the fact that all signals have variable delays since the transition time of LBDL gates is independent of input values. Results demonstrate that LBDL avoids the majority of leakage while maintaining similar performance and area costs to WDDL.

Wei Liu *et al.* (2014), With this research, a novel approach for reducing noise effects via wavelet analysis is given, with the goal of improving the performance of side-channel power attacks known as WPA (Wavelet-based Power Attack). On a widely available contact-less smart card based on 3DES, which is frequently used for security-sensitive applications, the key is obtained. WPA considerably enhances the success rate of encryption key detection, according to test results. A needed number of power traces is 50% smaller when compared to the fourth-order cumulant noise reduction approach for power attack.

Martin Petrvalsky *et al.* (2016), an innovative small hardware platform based on a microcontroller unit is provided for evaluating and developing power analysis side-channel attacks and implementations in this work. A correlation power analysis attack on a multi-precision multiplication, which is part of numerous cryptographic protocols such as an elliptic curve digital signature technique, is used to illustrate the system. First, the platform's fundamental features, benefits, and applications are considered. Following that, a measurement setup and attack tactics are given. Then, in terms of the attack, alternative implementations of multi-precision multiplication and their features are outlined. Finally, several major findings of the assault on the innovative platform are presented, along with a discussion of new features of safeguarding multi-precision multiplication implementations.

2.2 S – BOX DESIGN

Saleh Ibrahim (2020) a novel S-box method of construction is presented in this work, which is related to the concept of optimization algorithms. The suggested technique constructs randomized S-boxes and maximizes the nonlinearity of the each Boolean function under bijectivity constraints using a random-restart hill-climbing algorithm. The proposed algorithm substantially sped up the construction of S-boxes. The suggested method offers a better based on these three design objectives of dynamic S-boxes, namely cryptographic strength, dynamicity, and building speed, as looking at recent S-box construction methods. The suggested method generates a new dynamic 8 8 S-box with NLD112 every 118 milliseconds on average, but an NLD110 S-box may well be formed in 5.3 milliseconds, making it perfect for real-time applications. With NLD114, the suggested approach creates 8-8 S-boxes, which is among the most reported in the literature. It has been shown that how the proposed limited optimal formulation may be used to improve other S-box design standards. In particular, an approach is offered for optimizing an S-LAP box's while maintaining its NL and bijectivity.

Po-Chun Liu *et al.* (2009), Various S-box circuit topologies were first investigated in this article, with the twisted BDD with m=4 proving to be the most effective. On SMIC 0.18m and Chartered 0.35m CMOS technology, a fast SMS4 cipher VLSI implementation based on the twisted BDD S-box architecture was achieved, with maximum frequencies of approximately 200MHz and 100MHz, respectively.

Nabihah Ahmad *et al.*(2010), The Advanced Encryption Standard (AES) is one of the most widely used symmetric encryption algorithms, according to Nabihah Ahmad *et al.*(2011). The AES substitution box (S-box), which is the only non-linear structure in the system, dominates the hardware complexity. It is one of the most complicated and expensive parts of the system. Combinational logic architecture of S-Box is used in the proposed study, which is implemented on a Virtex II FPGA device. In order to reduce the time, the architecture uses a Boolean simplification of the logic function's truth table. Basic gates such as AND, NOT, OR, and multiplexer are used to construct the S-Box. The design, in theory, decreases overall latency and is efficient for applications that require high-speed performance. In terms of gate area, this approach is appropriate for FPGA implementation. Hardware, total area, and delay are all visible.

Christopher A Wood *et al.* (2015), a method for identifying cryptographically relevant S-box constructions using power mappings over GF (2n) and looking for composite-field representations that allow for low-area hardware implementations is described in this paper. This technique is used to locate 16-bit S-boxes that allow area-minimized implementations, motivated by a prospective requirement for larger S-boxes. This methodology and these findings could be valuable in the development of future cryptographic algorithms, according to us.

Rahaman *et al.* (2010) The S-box that is among the most important blocks in AES hardware implementation is presented in this report as a C-testable architecture. Tested subsequent orders an additional 15% of hardware. To ensure 100% testability of stuck-at faults, just 14 test vectors are used. We employed a BIST structure, which reduces the necessity for the three control inputs that also are required for S-box testing. For testability, the proposed design does not require a scan chain, eliminating the chip's vulnerability during testing. One can eliminate potential avenues for providing unauthorized access into the on-chip security blocks by introducing on-chip impacts.

Kaedi *et al.* (2019) in this paper, we present a fundamental analysis of the situation of flattening the power in D3C and analyze it with the help of counterexample. To execute an effective DPA attack, we used a non-true temporally random power like a flaw of the IOA countermeasure in the suggested technique. A chosen-plaintext attack is the attack technique. The input data pattern is set to be constant in this attempt to correct the D3C countermeasure's delay. As a result, the countermeasure is evaded, and the DPA attack on the S-box (the S-box) established by IOA is efficient. All of the bits of the S-box, which was stated to be attack-proof by the D3C approach, are retrieved bitwise by this attack. To begin, S-box is modeled in a SPICE simulator to carry out the proposed concept. After that, HDL experimental findings support the suggested assault on the IOA countermeasure. A Sakura-GW evaluation board and a Xilinx FPGA Spartan-6LX75 test-bed are used in the experiment.

Po-Chun Liu *et al.* (2010), the first-order DPA attack is effectively resisted using a DPA countermeasure circuit associated with digital controlled ring oscillators given in this short. The unique geographical of a single S-box is about 19 percent without any extra delay in the critical path, according to the execution of the crucial S-box of the advanced encryption standard (AES) algorithm. The countermeasure circuit can also be installed on other S-box method helped on composite fields or look-up tables (LUT). Depending on this methodology, a DPA-resistant AES device with fewer than 2K more gates may be offered to preserve almost same throughput.

Dinesh Kumar *et al.* (2018), this paper introduces FinSAL, a new FinFET-based Secure Adiabatic Logic which is both energy-efficient and DPA-resistant. Logic gates such as buffers, XOR, and NAND are developed using the recommended adiabatic FinSAL. A Positive Polarity Reed Muller (PPRM) architecture oriented S-box circuit is also developed using logic gates founded on adiabatic FinSAL. When compared with the conventional S-box circuit built using FinFETs, adiabatic FinSAL (20nm FinFET technology) S-box circuit saves up to 81 percent of energy each cycle, according to SPICE simulations at 12.5 MHz (20nm FinFET technology). Furthermore, the security of adiabatic FinSAL S-box circuit has been assessed using SPICE simulations and the DPA attack. Beyond a devised DPA attack flow suitable to SPICE simulations, we established that the FinSAL S-box circuit is resistant to a DPA attack. FinSAL's benefit on hardware security at multiple FinFET technology nodes (7nm, 10nm, 14nm, and 16nm) is also evaluated. As per the simulation results, FinSAL gates in 14nm FinFETs provide greater security while consuming the least amount of power, making them the greatest candidate for designing low-power secure IoT devices.

Moshe Avital *et al.* (2015), this study introduces a low-power, DPA-resistant secured quasi-adiabatic logic (SQAL) technique. The SQAL technology's efficiency was tested on an 8-bit AES-128 SBOX block and found to be resistant to DPA attacks. The SQAL technique offers better outcomes in terms of power consumption and area overhead when compared to alternative adiabatic and non-adiabatic logic styles.

Yiqun Zhang *et al.* (2018), this work offers Recryptor, a reconfigurable cryptographic processor that adds computing capabilities to an existing commercial general-purpose processor's memory. It uses a 10-transistor bit cell to provide several bitwise operations up to 512 bits wide in memory bit line computation. Close-memory computing capabilities are provided by custom-designed shifter, rotator, and S-box modules that reside near the memory. By implementing the cryptographic primitives of several public/secret key cryptographies and hash functions, we illustrate Recryptor's programmability. With only 0.128 mm2 area overhead in 40-nm CMOS, Recryptor runs at 28.8 MHz in 0.7 V, yielding 6.8 average speedup and 12.8 average energy savings over state-of-the-art software- and hardware-accelerated solutions.

Arash Reyhani-Masoleh *et al.* (2018), For the AES S-box, there are three new hardware designs that can be used in the forward, inverse, or mixed data pathways. In its respective categories, each of these designs represents the smallest AES S-box ever suggested. This aim can be achieved by optimizing each block within the three suggested designs using a novel tower field representation over normal bases. In both the CMOS STM 65nm and NanGate 15nm technologies, the complexity analysis and ASIC synthesis findings reveal that these designs outperform their rivals in terms of area and power.

Julia Juremi *et al.* (2012), A novel AES-like architecture for key dependent AES utilizing S-box rotation is suggested in this study. It has been explained that how to utilize this feature to make an S-box key-dependent and therefore make the AES stronger. The cipher structure is similar to the original AES, except that the S-box is made key-dependent without affecting the value. This new design will be put to the test using the NIST Statistical Test and then crypt examined with an algebraic attack to see whether it can be subverted or evaded.

Xiang dong Yin (2010), this research presents a tabu-genetic algorithm-based s-box optimization approach. A niche technique is used in the algorithm to sustain population variety and avoid premature convergence. Other attributes, such as s-box avalanche criteria and diffusion features, are used as evolution objectives, and box efficiency is investigated further. The experimental results indicated that generating an s-box with the modified tabu-genetic technique limitation of the research is possible and efficient. Furthermore, the new approach can not only provide a series of s-boxes with a high degree of nonlinearity and low differential evenness, but it can also severely reduce redundant calculations and accelerate convergence speed.

Ashwak Alabaichi *et al.* (2015), this article analyses and details the process of improving the AES algorithm, which includes the creation of dynamic S-boxes for the Advance Encryption Standard (AES). Because the resulting S-boxes are more dynamic and key-dependent, differential and linear cryptanalysis becomes more challenging. The suggested dynamic AES algorithm was subjected to NIST randomness tests and correlation coefficients, with the results demonstrating that it is superior to the original AES with security validated.

2.3 CRYPTOGRAPHY

Jia Wang *et al.* (2018), Multivariate public key cryptosystems founded on extended Clipped Hopfield Neural Networks (CHNN) will be presented, and they will be constructed using the MVC (CHNN-MVC) framework in GF(p) space. The Diffie–Hellman key exchange method is generalized into the matrix field, revealing the potential of new applications in both conventional and post quantum cryptography. CHNN-MVC, the proposed new public key cryptosystem, is simulated and found to be NP hard. The proposed method increases multivariate public key cryptosystems also while providing for embedded system.

Kimmo Järvinen & Jorma Skytta (2008) this paper will explain where parallelism should be utilized to improve effectiveness and offers methods for analyzing its use. A set of curves termed as Koblitz curves deserves special attention as they provide very effective point replication. With simultaneous field arithmetic processors, a novel method for minimizing point multiplication latency has already been presented. In the circumstances of Koblitz curves and generic curves with fixed base points, it exceeds the previously published multiple field multiplier methods. The design of a highly efficient universal elliptic curve cryptography processor is presented and explored. A few initiatives have been developed on an Altera Stratix II Field-Programmable Gate Arrays predicated on this architecture as well as an investigation of the implications of parallel processing.

Walid El-Shafai *et al.* (2021), this study presents an optical HEVC cryptography algorithm for secure and efficient multimedia communication applications that would be more secure against entrants and hackers. Use of the 2D-FrFT ciphering technique with the 3D-JST for building a reliable and practical optical HEVC cryptography algorithm seems to be the major involvement and impact of this research study. As a result, a proposed cryptography technique effectively adds extra diffusion and permutation to the ciphered HEVC frames. To establish its security and efficiency, the proposed approach was properly evaluated against a range of assessment metrics. The simulations results showed that the proposed optical cryptography outperformed relevant research in almost all measured metrics and in comparing to effectively ciphering streamed HEVC frames. As a result, it is better suited to securing video transmission than conventional cryptographic algorithms.

Adonis Bogris *et al.* (2008) During the first instance, the comeback phase of a chaotic system which contains a semiconductor laser exposed to delayed optical feedback is addressed as a secret key for secure chaotic communications that is not solely reliant on hardware uniqueness. Numerical simulations analysis shows that such feedback phase is essential for synchronization. Bit-error rate calculations numerically quantify an eavesdropper's capacity to intercept an intensity-modulated transmission whenever a pseudorandom change of the feedback phase is introduced at the transmitter's side. The research suggests that even though the eavesdropper is supplied with an identical chaotic device may be unable to synchronies and so extract the message if he is unaware of the phase variations.

Muhtahir O Oloyede & Gerhard P. Hancke (2016), this study gives a thorough examination of a various unimodal and multimodal biometric sensing types, as well as their benefits and drawbacks. It goes over the many stages of the biometric system recognition system, along with multimodal systems design, operation mode, and methodologies employed to design the devices. It also addresses many levels and methods of integration used during biometric systems, providing researchers a better grasp of multimodal biometric sensing and processing systems and also research trends therefore in domain. It also provides for research into how to find answers to problems with various unimodal biometric systems.

Alejandro Freyre-Echevarria *et al.* (2020), In this paper, a new hybrid method based on the Leaders and Followers and hill-climbing over Hamming Weight Classes met heuristics, and also a new trade-off fitness function that generates 8-bit bijective substitution boxes to excellent resistance to conventional cryptanalysis and side-channel attacks by power consumption is introduced. The top Pareto optimum solutions for non-linearity and confusion coefficient variance multi-objective planning are considered.

Musheer Ahmad *et al.* (2020), the virtues of chaotic map and algebraic groups are combined in this study to propose a hybrid technique for the production of cryptographically strong bijective substitution-boxes. The hybrid technique builds key-dependent dynamic S-boxes first that used a chaotic heuristic search strategy, and afterwards develops the S-boxes utilizing potent suggested algebraic group structures. To operate the initial search technique, this work provides a new better combination chaotic map. The algebraic group structures that have the potential to boost the cryptographic strength of produced S-boxes are discovered to augment the strength of created S-boxes. The suggested bijective S-boxes' strengths are quantified using performance evaluations based on conventional criteria. The experimental results, as well as comparisons with contemporary S-box research findings, support the suggested bijective S-boxes and hybrid generation method's efficacy and competence.

Zeeshan Kaleem & Kyunghi Chang (2016), This study examines user association concerns in multi-tier heterogeneous networks (HetNets) in order to prevent co-channel interference and offer load balancing for proactively loading users into mobile personal cells (mPC). Much of the previous material focused on the user association problem in HetNets with fixed tiny cells. Because of the fixed nature of tiny cells, the problem mentioned in the current literature is simple to examine. The mPC, rather than fixed tiny cells, is the subject of this research, which complicates the user association problem due to its mobility. The priority-based mPC user association (PS-UA) approach for load balancing and interference reduction in highly fluctuating PS long-term evolution systems is suggested in this paper. As per network load conditions and PS user priority, the suggested strategy improves the user-association problem by lowering call blocking probability (CBP). It also enhances the user signal-to-interference-and-noise ratio by using an upgraded inter cell interference coordination mechanism, which reduces interference to offloaded users even more. System-level simulations confirmed the suggested PS-UA strategy's validity, since it significantly lowers the CBP for PS users as compared to the traditional static user association technique.

Yu Sasaki &Yosuke Todo (2018), this work examines the security of LILLIPUT, a lightweight block cipher introduced in the IEEE Transactions on Computers in 2015. The Extended Generalized Feistel Network (EFGN) is used by LILLIPUT. The non-linear, linear, and permutation layers make up EGFN, and the linear layer only update a portion of the state linearly, which raises various security problems. The first finding is that the designers' bottom limitations for the number of differentially active S-boxes are erroneous. As a result, mixed integer linear programming (MILP) is used to calculate the new boundaries. Sun et al two-stage's search strategy has been used, which yields tight limits even for huge numbers of rounds. After that, the search tool is transformed into a linear cryptanalysis tool. The difficult challenge of assessing LILLIPUT's security against differential and linear cryptanalysis has been solved with these improvements. The finest third-party cryptanalysis is another contribution. EGFN was designed to effectively improve security against integral cryptanalysis, according to the creators. Security, on the other hand, is not as good as the designers had hoped. In reality, the division property produces a 13-round distinguisher, which is 4 rounds better than the prior distinguisher. The distinguisher is also expanded to a 17-round key recovery, which are 3 rounds better than the previous greatest attack.

Xiang Wang *et al.* (2014), this letter offers a lossless TVC system, which is an enhanced TVC scheme (LTVC). The term "lossless" refers to the fact that the proposed LTVC method encodes the tag picture without harming the reconstructed secret image, i. e., the decoded secret image of LTVC has the same visual quality as the conventional VC technique. Furthermore, we suggest the probabilistic LTVC (P-LTVC) to address the LTVC's possible security issue. Finally, the suggested scheme's advantage is demonstrated experimentally.

Dao-Shun Wang *et al.* (2013), we provide a new greyscalen RVCS with minimum pixel expansion and an optimal-contrast 40iphers4040 RVCS (GRVCS) based on the basis matrices of perfect black nRVCS in this work. In addition, even if the basis matrices are not fully black, an optimum GRVCS is offered. Finally, given a minimal number of shares held by each participant, we build an optimal-contrast GRVCS. Previous RVCSs for binary pictures may be considered as special instances in the schemes described here; previous RVCSs for binary images can be viewed as special cases in the schemes proposed here.

Satyanarayana Vollala *et al.* (2014), four techniques for evaluating modular exponentiation are presented in this paper. Bit forwarding (BFW) techniques are suggested to calculate an x mod n, and two algorithms, Substitute and reward (SRW), and Store and forward (SFW), are presented to compute an x b y mod n. All of the presented techniques are time efficient and need just a little amount of extra storage space to hold the pre-computed values. These methods are appropriate for devices with limited computing power and storage.

Zhenfei Zhang *et al.* (2008), a hitherto unexplored approach of using certificate less public key encryption (CL-PKE) techniques over mobile ad hoc network (MANET) is provided in this research. There are essentially two primary techniques in modern literature, including public key cryptography and identity-based (ID-based) cryptography. They both, however, have some inherent flaws. A certificate authority (CA) is required in a public key cryptography system to issue certificates between users' public keys and private keys to ensure their authenticity, whereas in an ID-based cryptography system, users' private keys are generated by a key generation centre (KGC), which means the KGC knows every user's keys (the key escrow problem). To overcome these challenges, Al-Riyami and Paterson developed certificate less cryptography systems, in which public keys are not required to be certified and the KGC is unaware of the users' keys. In essence, certificate less cryptography is a hybrid of public key and identity-based cryptography. The notion of Shamir's secret sharing technique is utilized to implement CL-PKE over MANET and make it feasible. Some or all of the MANET nodes share the master secret keys. Once the network has been established, this allows the system to self-organize. We explore both a full distribution system and a partial distribution system to give additional flexibility. In addition, two simulations has been run to back up the theories. To calculate the encryption, decryption, and key distribution efficiency, first simulation has been made. Then, to assess the network efficiency, AODV is used to emulate the scheme. The simulations are run on the OPNET network.

Shiny *et al.* (2016), this study offers a tagged visual cryptography technique for colour pictures, in which the secret image is divided into two base shares using a typical visual cryptography scheme. To acquire the tagged shares, the created base shares are stamped with the tag pattern using the probabilistic visual cryptography technique. One of the primary benefits of adopting tag patterns is that it provides participants with additional information to help them find the relevant shares from the many available. The tag patterns are created by folding up the individual labeled shares during reconstruction. When you superimpose the shares, you get a private colour image that keeps its original size, preventing pixel expansion.

2.4 EFFICIENT CHARGE RECOVERY LOGIC

Shravan *et al.* (2014), A revolutionary approach for power gating mechanism using Improved Efficient Charge Recovery Logic (IECRL) is reported in this section. Improved Efficient Charge Recovery Logic created the Asynchronous Fine-Grain Power-Gated Logic Technique (AFPLT), which provides logic function to the next step. IECRL gates in the AFPLT circuit receive power as from hand shaking controller only becoming activated whenever needed executions are executed. Permeability currents are controlled in aggressive state by providing an infinite resistance channel through NMOS transistor in the pull-up network. IECRL gates do not consume any power in inactive state, resulting in very low leakage power dissipation. At a 100 MHZ input data rate, it will save up to 82.8% more power than ECRL. At 100 MHZ, the savings are up to 92.68 percent as compared to static CMOS logic. The handshake encoder in the AFPLT circuit has been used to supply power to the IECRL gate and to execute handshakes with the bordering stages. A PCR mechanism is employed in the AFPLT basic concept in order to minimize energy dissipation. The charge of the discharging phase of an IECRL gate is transported to the analysis stage of that other IECRL gate using the PCR method. The improved C-element, known as the C*-element, can offer early IECRL gate discharge.

Subhashini & Geetha (2014), the goal of this study is to diminish the influence, area, and gateway counts. Asynchronous Coarse Grain Power Gated Logic (ACGPL) has already been applied in this research. The advantages of asynchronous circuits and combinational logic design are merged in this design. A stage of ACGPL pipeline is comprised of an adiabatic logic gate and a protocol controller. The handshake controller is often used to connect with surrounding devices and give power to logic gates, while the adiabatic logic gate performs the logical design of stage. In the ACGPL circuit, logic gates get power and become active only when they are performing valuable operations; idle data structures are not powered, leading in minimal leakage power dissipation. This paper can also incorporate the Partial Charge Reuse (PCR) mechanism, which is utilized to govern charge reuse between two stages. Asynchronous Coarse Grain Power Gated Logic (ACGPL) and Asynchronous Adiabatic Power Gated Logic (AAPGL) are compared in this study (AAPL). The main disadvantage of fine grain power gating is that adding a sleep transistor to every cell that needs to be turned off takes up a lot of space, and individually gating the power of each cluster of cells introduces timing issues that are difficult to resolve due to inter-cluster voltage variation. The "coarse-grain" sleep transistor implementation is preferred by most power-gating designs over the "fine-grain" variant, which has a huge space cost and higher PVT sensitivity.

Aarushi Mann1 *et al.* (2020), In the context of a two-input multiplexer relying on Efficient Charge Recovery Logic (ECRL), the influence of header and footer power gating strategies is evaluated. The power consumed by conventional adiabatic circuits has already been efficiently mitigated employing power gating processes. Simulations in Tanner tool employing 32 nm PTM models have been used to test the performance and profitability of circuits constructed with MUX. The impact of source voltage, load capacitance, and power clock signal frequency on power degradation is examined. The analysis shows that in the awake state, the header gated ECRL based MUX consumes higher power. Within idle state, but at the other hand, is there a large power reduction.

Keote & Karule (2015), improved framework for efficient charge recovery logic is described in this study. Low-power analysis is used across the designer, from subsystem to process level, to optimize the power dissipation of digital systems. Meanwhile, Efficient Charge Recovery Logic (ECRL) and recommended Efficient Charge Recovery Logic have been implemented in NAND and NOR gates. The inverter and basic gates are compared at transition frequencies ranging from 50MHz to 400MHz in this paper. When compared to normal circuits, the recommended circuits can save considerable amount of power. The circuits are simulated using nodes with a 180nm technology.

Willliam Morell & Ashok Srivastava (2018) in this paper, four specific power-clock gating techniques are analyzed and compared to be used with four-phase adiabatic logic in respect of idle power reduction and active power consumption enhancement. The simulations information is obtained with single buffer/inverter structures in efficient charge recovery logic (ECRL). Independent header and footer power-gating systems, but also regular digital and pulsed adiabatic logic-style control signals, have also been investigated. Tanner's T-SPICE software and 180nm CMOS technology were used to create all simulation data.

2.5 POSITIVE FEEDBACK ADIABATIC LOGIC

David J Willingham & Izzet Kale (2008) in this paper, it is been demonstrated that PFAL seems to have the capacity to enact any reversible logic function. It was further established that making PFAL completely reversible reduces power usage significantly. The possibility of constructing reversible pipelines using Asynchrobatic logic has been suggested, and it is obvious that more investigation is necessary.

Shiv Pratap Singh Kushawaha *et al.* (2015), in this paper, modified positive feedback adiabatic logic (MPFAL). MPFAL is powered by a positive DC voltage ranging from 0.1 to 0.45 volts. Cadence Virtuoso Tool had been used to construct updated PFAL circuits on UMC 180 nm CMOS technology. This modified procedure achieves INVERTER, NAND neither gate, NOR gate, and EX-NOR gate, and it is related to Positive Feedback Adiabatic Logic (PFAL). In evaluating an individual's approach to PFAL for input frequencies ranging from 10 to 500 MHz and simulations using 50 to 300 fF ranges of load capacitances, this is clear that the updated new functionalities lower average power. Higher frequencies were employed in this technology, which was utilized in ultra-low power digital devices. The transistor density is much like the PFAL.

Akash Agrawal *et al.* (2016) this paper aims at comparing the effectiveness of proposed adiabatic logic circuit, in terms of power dissipation, over other adiabatic logic families by simulating different logic gates using these logic families. All the simulations are done using HSPICE simulator at 65nm technology at different frequency range. Comparative results are presented by different bar graphs plotted at different frequencies, which shows least power dissipation for the proposed logic circuit.

Antonio Blotti *et al.* (2002) in this document with only one external inductor, a four phase PCG with positive feedback adiabatic logic is demonstrated. A simple examination of the technique offers closed form conclusions for design procedure. The effectiveness of the technique is confirmed by an error rate of less than 7% when compared to simulations. When compared to traditional CMOS systems that are functionally identical to adiabatic systems, the adiabatic systems save two to four times the energy.

Sonal Aron *et al.* (2015) this paper, A MUX decoder based on positive feedback adiabatic logic (PFAL) is suggested. The decoder was constructed using 180nm CMOS technology and SPICE simulation. In based on power dissipation, PFAL-based decoder exceeds the standard CMOS-based decoder. The described MUX decoder has attained a substantial reduction in power loss of 41.867 percent.

CHAPTER 3

HYBRID ENERGY RECOVERY LOGIC (HERL)

3.1 INTRODUCTION

The Internet of Things (IoT) is becoming more prevalent in everyday activities including home automation, elder care support, smart health care, transportation, agriculture, and environmental monitoring, among others. Smart cards, Subscriber Identity Module (SIM) cards, Radio Frequency Identification (RFID) tags, and other Integrated Circuit (IC)-based devices are used in these activities. These devices keep track of their users' personal information and then use it to communicate with them. As a result, a secure system must be designed that is resistant to side-channel attacks such as power analysis, timing attacks, and Differential Power Analysis (DPA) attacks. To be secure, user information must be encrypted and susceptible to hardware faults.

Encryption is an encoding method that converts one type of data into another, allowing only authorized individuals to access it throughout the decryption phase. To defend these cryptographic systems against DPA attacks, many techniques based on hiding and masking have been developed. Because these techniques are subject to DPA attacks, they have a high power consumption, which makes them unsuitable for practical applications like portable and mobile devices. The security of these gadgets is inverse proportion to the battery's lifespan, which is a critical parameter for mobile applications. To address these concerns, adiabatic logic is used, which is the most energy-efficient circuit design method.

With the AES algorithm, a security and reliability of smartcards and RFID tags are increased. AES is used in the majority of encryption techniques to improve data security and privacy. Sub Bytes, Shift Rows, Mix Columns, and Add Round Key are the four basic operations in AES. It takes 10 rounds for a 128-bit key, 12 rounds for a 192-bit key, and 14 rounds for a 256-bit key. Some vulnerability in the hardware implementation of the AES algorithm is emerged as a result of electromagnetic and side-channel attacks. CMOS technology is first used for AES implementation; however it is immune to DPA assaults. As a result, for cryptographic systems, adiabatic logic is preferable. However, ECRL is unable to do so.

3.2 PROPOSED HERL XOR DESIGN

The HERL XOR gate is formed by blending two adiabatic logics called ECRL and PFAL. The suggested XOR gate combines the ECRL and PFAL logic's pull-up networks. The general structure of the HERL XOR gate is shown in Figure 3.1.

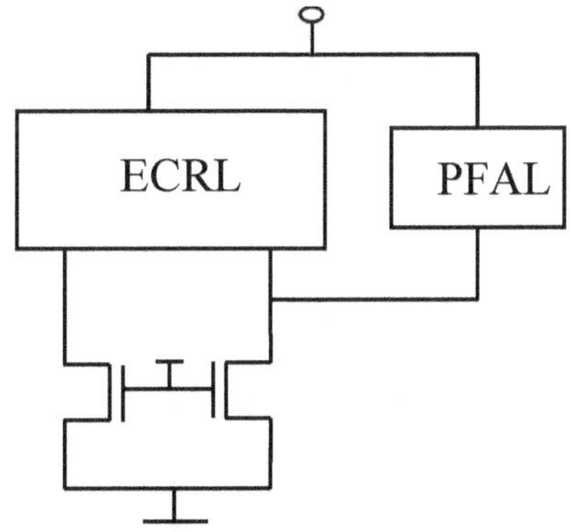

Figure 3.1 General Structure of Proposed HERL XOR Gate

Instead of cross-coupled inverters like PFAL, PMOS transistors are cross-coupled like ECRL in this proposed logic. When compared to conventional adiabatic circuits, the suggested logic consumes less energy. This logic is used to create an XOR gate, which can be used to create a secure S-Box. The schematic diagram of the proposed HERL XOR gate is shown in Figure 3.2.

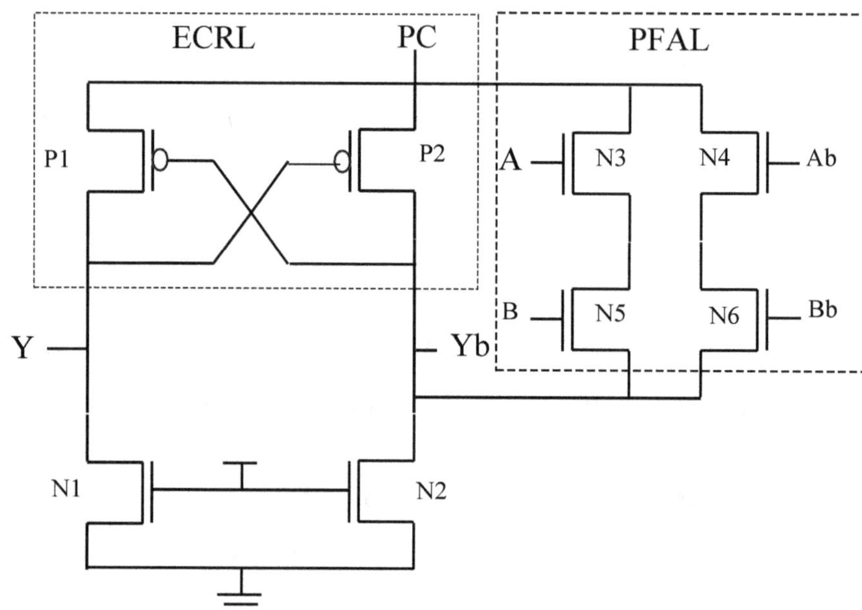

Figure 3.2 Schematic Diagram of Proposed HERL XOR gate

The proposed HERL XOR gate's inputs are indicated by A, B, and complementary inputs are denoted by Ab, Bb. The output is denoted by Y, Yb. PC is a power clock that functions as a power supply and has four modes: evaluation, wait, hold, and recovery. Because the power clock PC is set to '1' in recovery mode, it acts like a regular XOR gate. Within pull-up network, P1, P2 denotes PMOS transistors, whereas N3, N4, N5, N6 denotes NMOS transistors. As in pull-down network, N1, N2 denotes NMOS transistors. Because the gate inputs are coupled to the supply voltage Vdd, the transistors N1 and N2 are constantly conducting. If the suggested design's inputs are comparable, the circuit's response is low, and if any of the inputs is high, the circuit's output reaction is high.

3.3 CMOS INVERTER

The CMOS inverter has a non-adiabatic characteristic in normal operation. CL will be charged to VDD if the transistor M1 is initially turned on due to a low condition at the input. If finally the input moves to high, M1 will turn off, trapping the charge now at output. M2 will be turned on by the input data. A discharge channel for CL will show once M2 begins conduction. When this occurs, the charge that had been trapped in CL will be dissipated to ground.

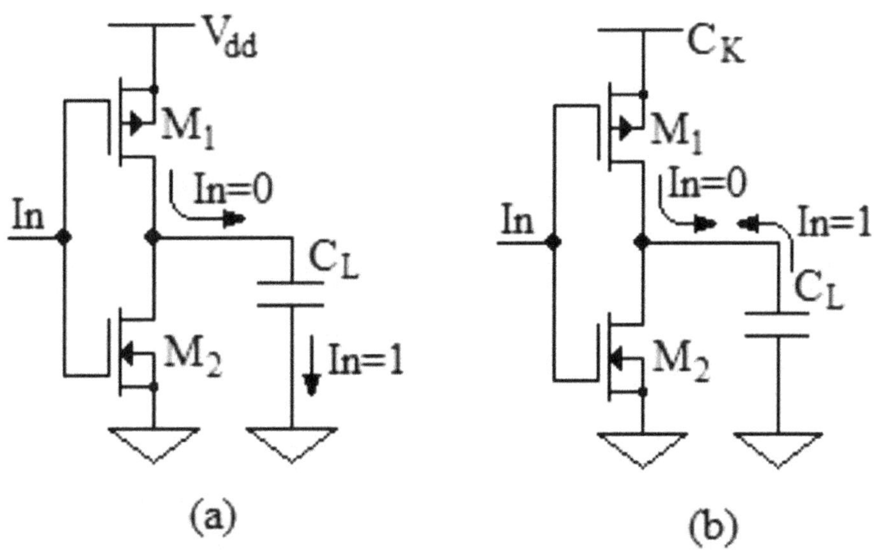

Figure 3.3 (a) non adiabatic behaviour (b) adiabatic behaviour

Adiabatic operation can be achieved using a CMOS inverter in the same circuit. To allow energy recovery, the adiabatic inverter uses a sinusoidal clock as a power supply instead of a DC voltage source. The power clock (Ck) starts at zero and gradually increases to its maximum value. M1 begins conduction in the situation where the input is zero. CL is fully charged and a high state is set at the output once Ck reaches VDD. If the low condition at the input persists, M1 continues to operate even as Ck approaches zero, pulling the charge back to the source. M1 never turns on in the case of a high input; hence there is no charge to be recovered from the load. The status of the input must remain constant during the load-charge and energy-recovery periods. If the input changes throughout these operations, the state at the output may become ambiguous, or energy may be lost.

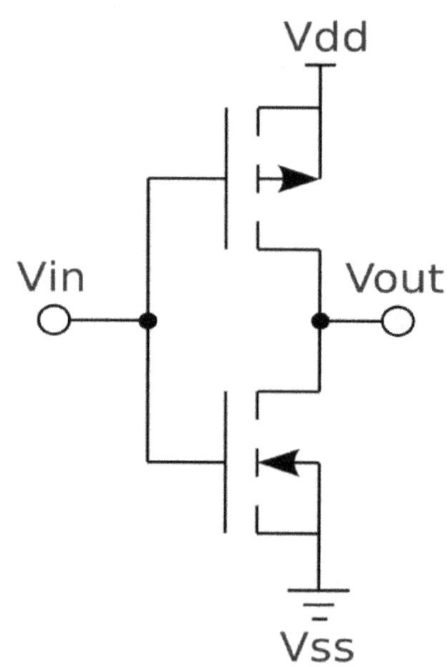

Figure 3.4 CMOS Inverter

To achieve adiabatic behaviour, the power supply must progressively vary from its lowest to highest value and vice versa. A transistor can be thought of as a resistor that dissipates non-recoverable static power. If the power clock changes too quickly, the voltage between drain and source (VDS) can become large enough to cause static dissipation losses. Because static dissipation is proportional to the frequency of operation, even if an adiabatic circuit can function quicker, the frequency must be kept artificially low.

3.4 EFFICIENT CHARGE RECOVERY LOGIC

Efficient Charge Recovery Logic (ECRL) is one of the most often used adiabatic techniques, with a structure consisting of two cross-coupled PMOS transistors M1 and M2 and two NMOS transistors connected in parallel to the N-functional blocks or N-tree for the ECRL adiabatic logic realization. The functional blocks are made entirely of NMOS transistors. The ECRL gates are powered by a pulsed power supply, which allows the energy to be collected and reused. To successfully recover the energy given by the supply clock, ECRL additionally employs four–phase power clocking. The subsequent clock pulses have a phase difference of 900, requiring the next stage to evaluate the logic values in the idle and evaluate phases when the preceding stage is in hold mode. ECRL is one of the popular adiabatic logic technique used which offers complimentary outputs and reduces the design complexity. As discussed before, Symmetric stacking based 6:3 compressor circuit involves blocks of full adder (FA), and half adder (HA), and hence the same is designed using ECRL aided ultra-low power adiabatic logic. An ECRL based sub-threshold biased adiabatic logic is applied on 8×8 multiplier circuit which involved symmetric stacking based 6:3 compressor subsystems.

The ultra-low power 6:3 symmetric stacked compressors is investigated using ECRL modified adiabatic logic circuits in the sub-threshold regime, and the system is extended to an 8:8 multiplier subsystem. The power savings are confirmed by the new symmetric stacked 6:3 compressor module. When compared to other adiabatic multiplier systems, the symmetric stacking technique eliminates the XOR computation from the critical path of the partial product reduction stage, boosting the circuit's performance. The average power consumption of the multiplier and 6:3 compressors in the range of nW and pW is investigated by adjusting the rail frequency, supply rise time, and load capacitances.

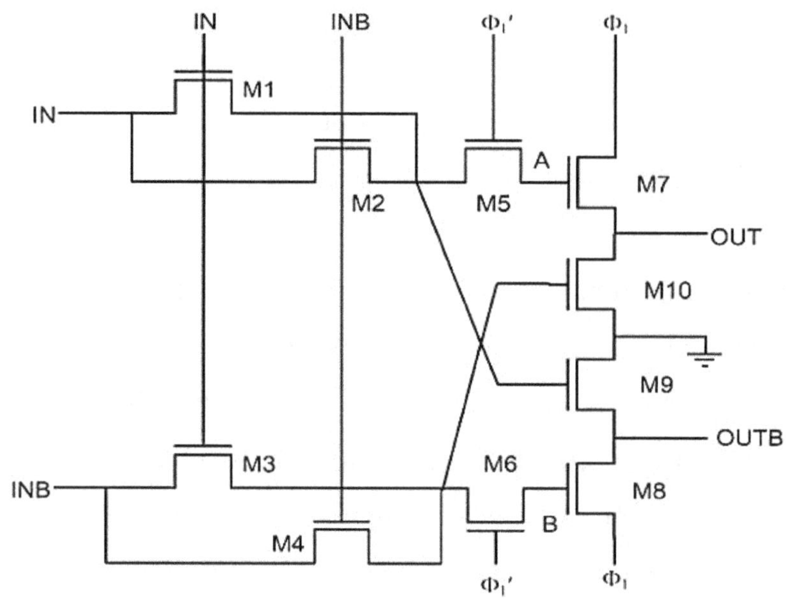

Figure 3.5 Efficient Charge Recovery Logic

The power profile indicated that supply parameters are sensitive to ultra-low power designed compressor and multiplier circuits, but that changes in load capacitances caused very little change in power consumption. The proposed improved multiplier design is well suited to biomedical applications requiring ultra-low power.

On the basis of power dissipation and transistor count, four-bit comparator circuits in CMOS, ECRL, and PFAL have been constructed and evaluated. The 4-bit ECRL comparator is 13.64 percent more efficient in power dissipation than 4-bit CMOS comparator, according to simulation studies, while the 4-bit PFAL comparator is 54.54 percent more efficient in power dissipation than 4-bit CMOS comparator. As a result, at 167 Hz, adiabatic filters are more efficient in terms of power dissipation as well as transistor count than CMOS comparators.

3.5 DIFFERENTIAL POWER ANALYSIS (DPA)

An exploit based on a correlation between the power usage of a chip in a smart card and the encryption key it holds is known as a differential power analysis attack. DPA attacks employ statistical analysis to get over countermeasures like extra noise, which is designed to disguise individual bits, by measuring power across several areas of the chip. When a device's power consumption is measured, it's possible to infer what kind of computational tasks it's doing. At this point, an analysis will reveal many bits of the crypto key, and the technique will be continued until the entire key is retrieved.

DPA attacks are risky because hackers bypass all supplier-installed hardware and software security measures. An intruder can compromise an embedded system without leaving traces since such attacks are non-invasive. To prevent DPA assaults, experts advise businesses to deploy smart cards that create a new key at random from the previous one each moment a card is used, rendering recorded keys useless. The Exclusive OR (XOR) gate is a key component in AES architecture. It is built utilizing HERL logic, which is resistant to DPA attacks and consumes less power than existing adiabatic logic designs. S-Box, which is an initial procedure in cryptographic protocols, is constructed with the help of this DPA resistant XOR gate. It resists DPA assaults with low energy usage and high security since it leveraged HERL XOR. The following is the research's contribution:

- HERL logic-based XOR gate design to improve power consumption by lowering the number of transistors.

- S-Box design with HERL-based XOR gate to boost cryptography application security.

3.6 FUNDAMENTALS OF ADIABATIC LOGIC

Adiabatic logic minimizes energy loss during the charging and discharging process. The term adiabatic is derived from the Greek word ‘adiabatos,’ which refers to state transitions that occur without the loss of heat. Charging and discharging occur at a steady current during these switching processes, resulting in little power consumption. Reduced power dissipation with variable switching activity is the property behind adiabatic switching. Because of the delayed transitions, the heat does not evaporate rapidly in this logic. It is possible to achieve this by employing an AC power supply rather than a DC power supply. The following mathematical equation is used to calculate total energy dissipation in adiabatic switching. It can be calculated in two different ways.

$$E_d = I^2RT = \left(\frac{CV_{dd}}{T}\right)^2 RT = \left(\frac{RC}{T}\right) CV_{dd}^2, \; T >> RC \tag{3.1}$$

$$E_d = \left(\frac{1}{2}\right) CV_{dd}^2, \; T << RC \tag{3.2}$$

Where R is resistance, T is time period, C is capacitance and Vdd is the supply voltage. Total energy dissipated as heat in adiabatic logic is computed by the following equation

$$E_T = E_{charge} + E_{discharge} \tag{3.3}$$

Maximum Power consumption of the XOR gate using various adiabatic logic XOR gate is shown in Figure 3.6. The proposed HERL logic reduces the power consumption by 7.75%, 21.12%, 15.51%, 8.18%, 7.67% and 3.87% when compared with existing adiabatic logic techniques such as ECRL, PFAL, DCB PFAL, Modified SQAL, 2N-2N2P and IDPAL.

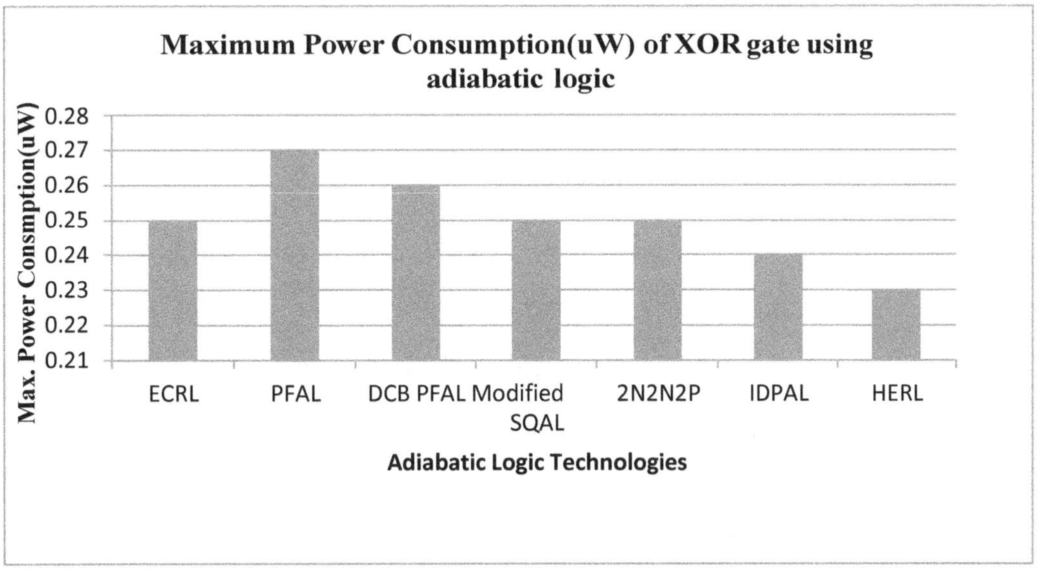

Figure 3.6 Maximum Power consumed by adiabatic logic XOR gate

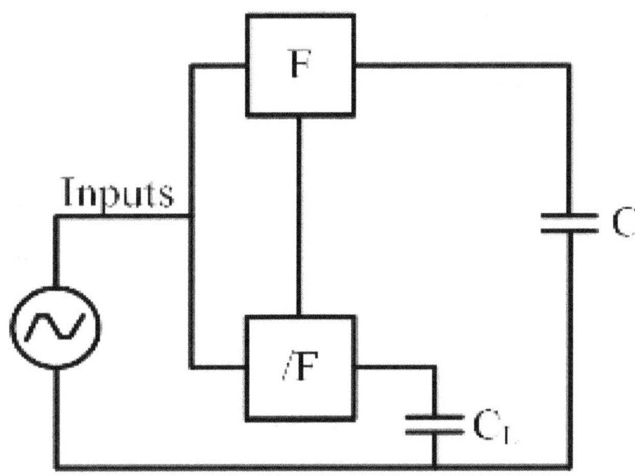

Figure 3.7 Adiabatic Logic Circuit

Transistor sizing, technology scaling, and power gating have all been used only to reduce power dissipation in adiabatic circuits. The topic of power gating is explored in this research study, which is a method of turning circuits off or putting circuits to sleep or idle while they are not in use. To achieve power gating, the circuit is separated from any of the power rails by placing sleep state control transistors between the circuit and the power rails.

While the sleep transistors are inactive, a power supply from across the function block collapsed towards the middle. As a consequence, the voltage change across the transistor gate, source, and drain is reduced, reducing leakage significantly.

Dynamic power dissipation accounts for 90% of overall power dissipation. Designers can decrease node capacitance, eliminate switching occurrences, reduce voltage swing, or spread grouping of these to reduce dissipation. However, before power dissipation, all of these ways consume the energy taken from the power supply once. Energy efficiency of logic circuits could be improved by introducing recycling of energy taken from the power source. Adiabatic Logic Circuits are a type of circuit that allows you to reuse energy from the supply while also lowering energy consumption while switching. The energies held in capacitance are utilized rather than being released as heat in this logic. Energy recovery CMOS seems to be another word for this. It is possible to obtain very low power dissipation in the circuit by just switching transistors under specific conditions and slowing the switching process.

3.7 POSITIVE FEEDBACK ADIABATIC LOGIC

The category of Positive Feedback Adiabatic Logic (PFAL) belongs to the adiabatic logic family. In comparison to other families such as ECRL, 2N-2N2P, and CAL, this PFAL uses the least amount of energy. It is resistant to progress in terms of technological parameters. The adiabatic amplifier at the core of PFAL is a latch made up of two nMOS and two pMOS. The two n-trees provide reliable logic functions and can provide both positive and negative outputs, depending on the situation.

The adiabatic methodology is a low-power, high-efficiency method for constructing logic circuits. Instead of being dissipated as heat, power dissipation at load capacitance might be recycled using this logic. In addition, the power dissipation in the pMOS network has been reduced. The output energy of CMOS logic circuits is totally drawn from the power source, i. e. energy stored at the load capacitor. With inverter NAND and NOR circuits, the suggested two logic families, ECRL and PFAL are compared to conventional CMOS logic.

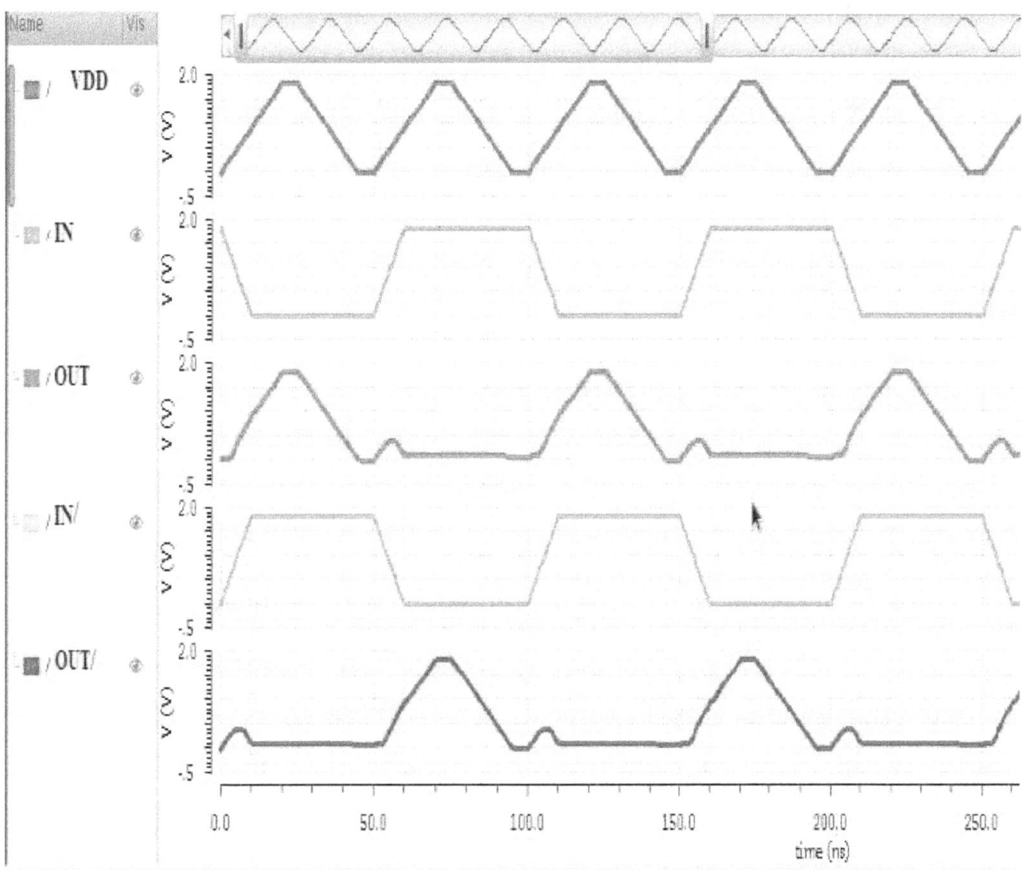

Figure 3.8 Waveform of modified PFAL INVERTER at 50 fF load capacitance for 10 MHz frequency at 0.1 V_{dc}. [37]

When power dissipation is a main concern, PFAL is a very useful approach. The peak power dissipation of the mux based decoder is decreased by 29.876 mw when the PFAL adiabatic approach is used in the implementation of mux, which is the only logic cell used in this mux based decoder. In reality, this reduction in power consumption should aid low-power, high-performance flash analogue to digital converters that use these mux-based decoders for thermometer to binary code conversion.

The PFAL method is a new adiabatic method that employs positive feedback. This logical structure is made up of cross-coupled inverters connected by NMOS devices between the yields as well as the power-clock. Pulse voltage signal, also known as power clock, is used in PFAL and is divided into four phases. The yields are evaluated during the Evaluation phase using stable information flags. Next the yield is held stable during the Hold interval, followed by the Recover Interval, that restores vitality, and finally, the outputs are embedded for symmetry during the Wait Interval. PFAL is a pair of double rail circuits that detect reciprocal contributions and provide yields that are complemented by incomplete vitality recovery.

As with PFAL operation, the current proposal features four phases for operation, which are quite similar to PFAL operation. Evaluation, Hold, Recover, and Wait are the four phases. 'ina' and 'inb' should have distinct voltage values during the evaluation stage, and equivalent NMOS devices should be conducted, resulting in corresponding outputs at the output levels 'outa' and 'outb'. A pulse voltage clock with two separate times is used in this scenario. The output will remain stable during Hold state until another clock is raised. The next phase is the recovery phase, in which the device strives to have the best possible performance from the input. Finally, while in Wait state, the output stays unchanged until the next operation is performed. During the operation, the four phases operate in sequence and provide the intended results.

In terms of power dissipation, the proposed PFAL design is more over 80% of Modified PFAL while 30% of Conventional PFAL, and in terms of delay, it is 20% more than Modified PFAL. So, based on these findings, It is concluded that our design is suitable, with PFAL play a critical role in terms of speed and power dissipation, and capable of providing superior performance. In the future, it is planned to expand our idea by creating an application based on it, and also attempting to implement it in hardware.

Positive feedback is used in the PFAL logic family, which is a relatively new logic family. These logic circuits have dual–rail in nature, allowing for partial energy recovery. The general block diagram illustrates how PFAL logic can be used to create a logic gate. An adiabatic amplifier, made up of a latch made up of two NMOS transistors (M3, M4) as well as two PMOS transistors, is at the core of Positive Feedback Adiabatic Logic (M1, M2). This latch is used to prevent logic level degradation at the output nodes (out and /out). Two n- trees are used to realize the complementary output functions (out and /out).

The functional nodes are interconnected in parallel to an adiabatic amplifier's PMOS, providing a transmission gate with lower equivalent resistance during capacitance charging. A pulsed power supply is used by PFAL. Idle, evaluate, recover, and hold are the four stages that make up this power supply. The in and /in input signals are at high and low levels, respectively. When the power clock climbs from low (0) to high (VDD) at the start of a cycle, the output (out) remains at ground (0) and the complementary output (/out) flows power via F. (n-tree). The output is valid logic by the time the power clock changes to VDD. During the hold phase, these output values are not changed and are fetched as inputs for the succeeding stages. Following the hold stage, the complementary output (/out) returns its energy to the power clock as it approaches zero, allowing the delivered charge to be recovered.

3.8 RESULTS AND DISCUSSION

S-Box with HERL logic is designed and simulated using Tanner EDA with 125nm technology. The efficiency of the proposed HERL XOR and S-Box are analyzed in terms of area, power consumption, delay and energy consumption.

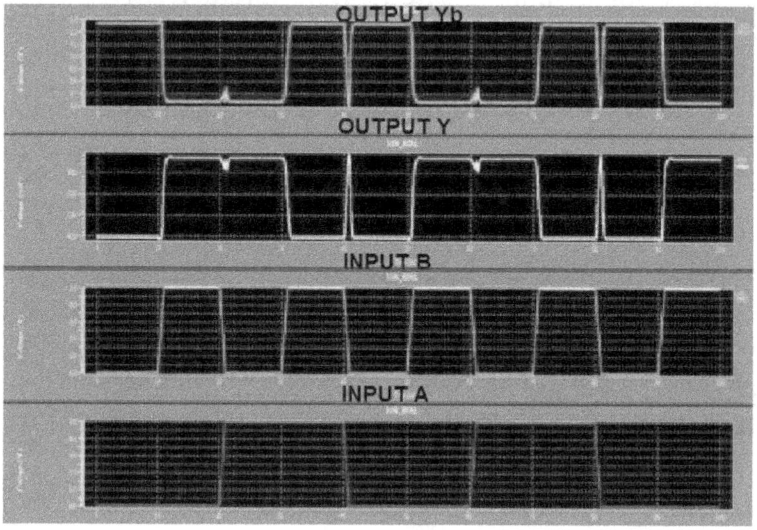

Figure 3.9 Simulation Waveform of proposed HERL XOR gate

To analyze the DPA resistance of the circuit, several inputs are applied to the S-Box design. Figure 3.9 shows the simulation result of the suggested HERL S-Box. A transient study of the HERL XOR gate is shown in this simulated waveform. The XOR gate's inputs are v(a), v(b), and its outputs are v(y), v(yb). The suggested HERL XOR gate's complementary output is v(yb).

The number of transistors in the proposed HERL XOR gate is the same as in ECRL logic. When compared to PFAL, EE-SPFAL, and IDPAL logic, it reduces the number of transistors by 33.33 %. When compared to DCBPFAL, M-SQAL, and 2N-2N2P logic, it also cuts the area down by 41.66 percent, 8.33 percent, and 16.66 percent, respectively. The average power consumption and delay of various adiabatic logic techniques are tabulated in Table 3.1.

Table 3.1 Delay and Power analysis of XOR gate using Adiabatic Logic Techniques

Technique	Delay (ns)	Average power (uW)	Energy Consumption (pJ)
ECRL [1]	0.07	4.165145	0.29156
PFAL [3]	0.11	4.165201	0.45816
DCDB PFAL [3]	0.11	4.16515	0.45816
2N-2N2P [3]	0.07	4.165205	0.29150
IDPAL [3]	0.14	4.165155	0.58312
HERL [Proposed]	0.07	4.165116	0.29155

From the tabulated results it is observed that ECRL, 2N-2N2P and the proposed HERL logic XOR has same delay as 0.07ns. The proposed HERL XOR reduces the delay by 57.14% when compared with PFAL and DCB PFAL. The Proposed HERL XOR gate consumed the power as 4.165116 uW lesser than other existing adiabatic logic techniques.

3.9 ANALYSIS OF PROPOSED HERL XOR GATE

The area of the proposed XOR gate is analyzed in terms of the number of transistors and it is compared with existing adiabatic logic techniques that is shown in Figure 3.10.

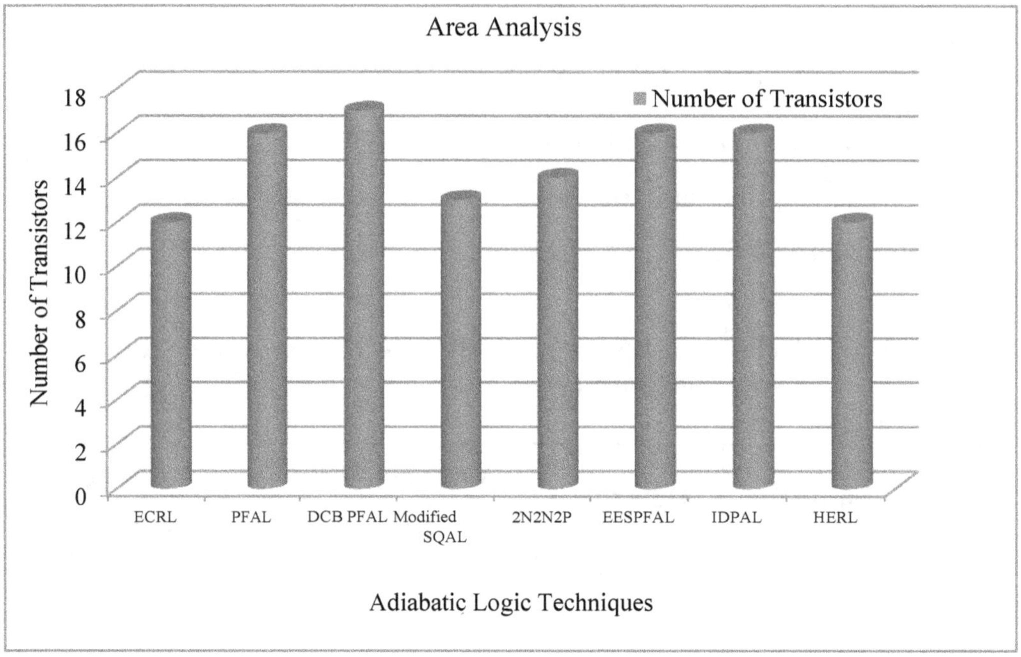

Figure 3.10 Area Analysis of Proposed HERL XOR gate

3.10 CONCLUSION

Energy-efficient 8-bit S-Box is designed for cryptography applications. It is designed using HERL logic which is vulnerable to DPA and this logic is obtained by merging ECRL logic and PFAL logic. The proposed HERL XOR gate is designed and simulated using Tanner EDA with 125 nm technology.

The proposed HERL XOR gate reduces the power consumption by 7.75%, 21.12%, 15.51%, 8.18%, 7.67% and 3.87% when compared with existing adiabatic logic techniques such as ECRL, PFAL, DCB PFAL, Modified SQAL, 2N-2N2P and IDPAL. The proposed S-Box design with HERL logic reduces the energy consumption by 35.14%, 42.17%, 30.67% and 10.46% when compared with the previous techniques such as ECRL, PFAL, DCB PFAL, 2N-2N2P and IDPAL.

3.11 SUMMARY

Hybrid Energy Recovery Logic (HERL) which combines two adiabatic logic techniques termed as Efficient Charge Recovery Logic (ECRL) and Positive Feedback Adiabatic Logic (PFAL). It is suitable for the S-Box design which is applicable for security applications. The proposed HERL XOR gate reduces the area by 41.66%, 8.33% and 16.66% when compared with Diode Connected DC Biased PFAL (DCDB-PFAL), Modified Secured Quasi Adiabatic Logic (M-SQAL) and 2N-2N2P logic. The proposed S-Box design with HERL XOR reduces the power consumption by 4.41%, 3.22%, 2.52%, 3.14% and 1.01% when compared with ECRL, PFAL, DCDB-PFAL, 2N-2N2P and Input Decoupled Partially Adiabatic Logic (IDPAL).

CHAPTER 4

GATED HYBRID ENERGY RECOVERY LOGIC (GHERL)

4.1 INTRODUCTION

Electronic device power consumption is increased as operational frequency and device performance are increased. There have never been a greater number of portable applications needing low power and high throughput than there has been in recent years. Furthermore, in the case of portable devices, high performance, light weight, and long operating duration are the primary design considerations, all of which are contradictory goals. The minimum feature size has been reduced significantly as a result of rising customer demand for efficient and low-power portable electronic products. Any drop in supply voltage will, without a doubt, result in a large reduction in overall power consumption, but it will also increase sub-threshold leakage and create unwanted sacrifices in physical capacitance and switching frequency. As a result, new designs and material paradigms have begun to emerge across the semiconductor device spectrum.

Low-power digital system design, particularly the fundamental blocks, is becoming as critical as high-performance system design. At low frequencies, the energy recovery logics circuits offer a significant reduction in power usage over static XOR. Because energy-recovery logic reuses charge, it requires less power than non-energy-recovery logic. Rather than draining charge to ground, an energy recovering logic charges the load capacitance during logic high to operate the gates. The charge injected to the load capacitance during logic level high is drained to ground at logic level low in non-energy recovering logic. The semiconductor industry's expansion is requiring designers to focus on smaller silicon areas, faster speeds, longer battery life, and dependability. In the recent decade, the semiconductor industry has seen tremendous growth in multimedia-based applications, as can be seen in laptops, cell phones, sensors, smart cards, and a variety of other products. In most of these applications, the exclusive OR (XOR) logic gate is a part of the critical path, which has a substantial impact on the system's worst-case latency and overall performance. The XOR gates are important components in a variety of digital systems, including arithmetic and logic circuits, crypto processors, test pattern generators, parity checks, and comparators, among others. As a result, enhancing the XOR gate's performance adds to a higher overall system performance.

Area, performance, cost, and reliability were formerly important concerns for VLSI designers. However, in recent years, this is beginning to change; power is increasingly being given equal weight to area and speed factors. There are a variety of approaches for lowering the power consumption of VLSI circuits. These can range from low-level steps like lowering the supply voltage or utilizing a higher threshold voltage to high-level methods like clock-gating or power-down modes. Energy recovery reasoning was the driving force behind this work. The ever-increasing need for portable applications such as mobile phones and laptops prompted designers to make considerable efforts to achieve high speed, longer battery life, and excellent dependability in a smaller silicon area. Adders, comparators, multipliers, parity generator/checkers, code converters, and error controlling coders, to name a few, all use the XOR as a basic building block. As a result, it's found in a lot of VLSI systems as part of the critical path, which defines the system's overall performance.

The complex logic's performance is determined by the performance of the individual XOR blocks that make it up. For XOR circuits to provide complete rail-to-rail swing, expend less power, and have reduced latency in the critical path and component economy, careful design and analysis are necessary. Different types of symmetric and asymmetric encryption methods are used to provide excellent security in wireless applications. However, due to limitations in the avalanche effect and IoT networks, some cryptographic methods are not suitable for network security. Asymmetric cryptography algorithms and several symmetric cryptography cipher techniques such as HEIGHT and RC5 are not suitable for IoT security because to their processing cost. Symmetric techniques like IDEA and the Advanced Encryption Standard (AES) can be used for IoT security, but they add to the computational complexity and power consumption.

4.2 ENERGY RECOVERY

Energy Recovery (ER) is a circuit design technique in which the charge in the load capacitor is recycled. It is possible to do so using adiabatic logic. Power gated techniques are recommended for additional energy and power dissipation reduction. The simple diagram of Gated Hybrid Energy Recovery Logic (GHERL) was shown in figure 4.1. In IoT applications, circuits should be extremely secured and energy efficient. It should also be resistant to DPA (Differential Power Analysis) assaults. Because of its high power consumption and vulnerability to DPA attacks, the CMOS IC architecture is not suited for real-time security applications.

To address these concerns, adiabatic logic is utilized, which has lower power dissipation than traditional methods. The S-Box in AES uses adiabatic logic and power gating to increase security and energy efficiency in real-time applications such as smart cards. To make the architecture as secure and resilient as possible, S-Box uses a Gated Hybrid Energy Recovery Logic

(GHERL) based XOR gate. Power gating is a technique for reducing power dissipation by interrupting the circuit's current flow.

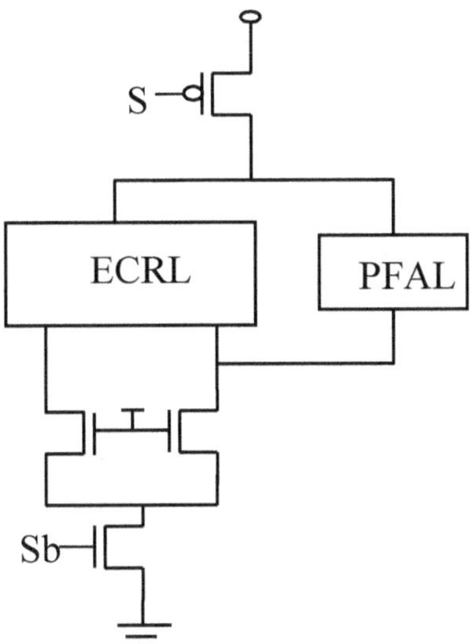

Figure 4.1 Gated Hybrid Energy Recovery Logic (GHERL)

To address these flaws in IoT security, our research focuses on the S-Box architecture, which is a key component of AES symmetric encryption. The XOR gate is used to construct every calculation in the S-Box structure. The XOR gate is a GHERL XOR gate that uses adiabatic logic and power gating to improve power consumption by lowering the number of transistors. To demonstrate the efficiency of the suggested design, its performance is compared in terms of area, delay, power consumption, and energy usage.

4.3 SIDE-CHANNEL ATTACK

Cryptography is primarily used to safeguard data and secure communication from outsiders and adversaries. It can encrypt and decode original and coded data. The secret key is used for both encryption and decryption. A cryptosystem is a system that conducts both encryption and decoding. Cryptanalysis is the process of determining how the secret key is produced from the leaked information. A side-channel attack (SCA) is a type of security hack that aims to harvest information from a chip or system. This can be accomplished by the measurement or analysis of numerous physical properties. Supply current, execution time, and electromagnetic emission are a few examples. These attacks are extremely dangerous to modules that combine cryptographic systems. Many side-channel analysis approaches have proved effective in cracking an algorithmically resistant cryptographic operation and retrieving the secret key. Figure 4.2 shows a block diagram of SCA. Various assaults are used by the attackers, including brute force attacks, SCA, and so on. Simple Power Analysis (SPA), DPA, and Correlation Power Analysis (CPA) are the three types of SCA. The secret key is hacked by SCA using the physical implementation of the devices. Light, sound, heat, electromagnetic radiation, time, power dissipation, and other responses from the system are possible. Because the focus of this study was on low power, leakage data was interpreted as power dissipation.

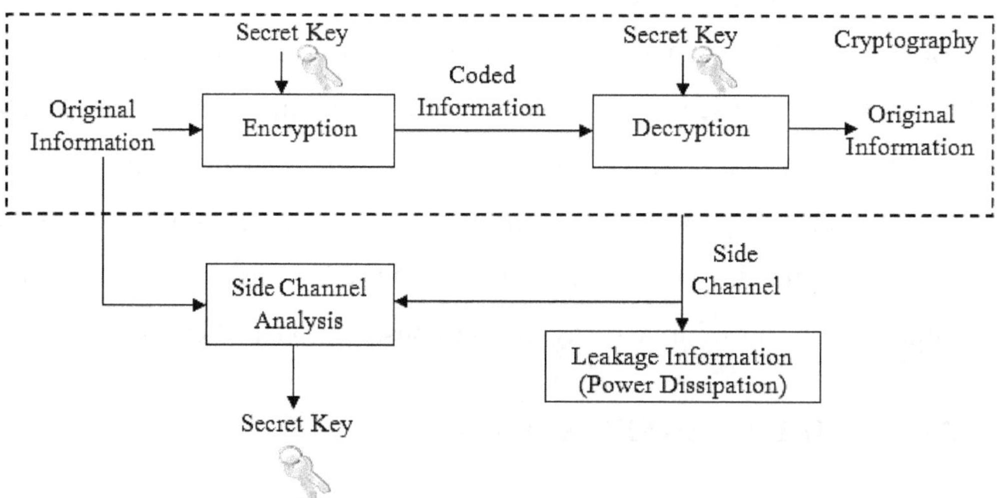

Figure 4.2 Side-Channel Attacks

To figure out the secret key, the adversaries employ SCA to deduce the link between these parameters and the system's operation. The information is released through a route capable of attacking the cryptosystem, known as SCA. The secret key is derived by comparing the leakage information collected from the side channels with the original information. Information leakage as a result of power dissipation may be reduced with the aid of GHERL XOR gate based S-Box design to safeguard the information from attackers.

4.4 GHERL BASED XOR

One type of leakage information in cryptography applications is the amount of power consumed. There is a requirement for low-power designs in order to convey information with great security. GHERL logic is a hybrid of adiabatic and power gating logic. The hybrid energy recovery logic (HERL) utilized here is a combination of Efficient Charge Recovery Logic (ECRL) and Positive Feedback Adiabatic Logic (PFAL). Figure 4.3 depicts the overall construction of a GHERL-based XOR gate.

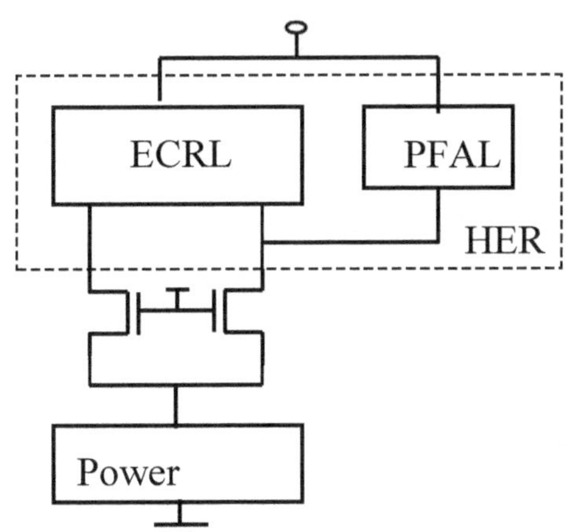

Figure 4.3 General Structure of GHERL XOR gate

One type of leaking information in cryptography applications is power consumption. There is a requirement for designs with minimal power consumption in order to transport information with good security. GHERL logic combines adiabatic logic with power gating. The adiabatic logic employed here is a Hybrid Energy Recovery Logic (HERL), which is a hybrid of Efficient Charge Recovery Logic (ECRL) and Positive Feedback Adiabatic Logic (PFAL). Figure 3 depicts the overall construction of a GHERL-based XOR gate.

4.4.1 Efficient Charge Recovery Logic (ECRL)

Efficient charge recovery logic (ECRL) is a standard logic style explored from adiabatic common sense that is more power efficient than typical CMOS circuits and has also been used in several sequential circuits. It employs a novel approach that accomplishes both pre-charge and evaluation at the same time. The ECRL circuit removes the pre-charge diode and uses less energy than conventional adiabatic circuits. To demonstrate the usefulness of this strategy, an ECRL inverter chain and a pipelined carry look-ahead adder (CLA) are built.

4.4.1.1 Basic operations of ECRL

The circuit structure of this logic is the same as that of 70iphers voltage switch logic (CVSL) with differential signaling. For the sake of this explanation, Assume that in is high and inb is low. When the supply clock φ_1 climbs from zero to V_{dd} at the start of a cycle, out stays at a ground level because the in signal switches on MN2. φ_1 is followed by $outb$ through MPI. The outputs are valid logic levels when φ_1 hits V_{dd}. Figure 4.4 depicts the schematic of the ECRL inverter.

These data are kept during the hold phase and utilized as inputs for the next stage's evaluation. When φ_1 descends to a ground level after the hold phase, outb node releases its energy to φ_1, allowing the given charge to be recovered. As a result, the clock φ_1 serves as both a clock and a power supply. For clock symmetry, a wait phase is added. In the previous stage, legitimate inputs are being prepared for this stage. A clocking rule is used to create a chain of logic circuits. To properly recover the charge given by the supply clock, ECRL employs four-phase clocking. With a 90° phase lag, each clock is followed by the preceding clock. As a result, while the previous stage is in the hold phase, the following stage must assess logic values in the pre-charge and evaluation phases. The simulated results for an ECRL inverter with SPICE in 0.5m CMOS technology are shown in Figure 4.5. In ECRL, the peak value of all supply clocks is set to 3V, the load capacitances are set to 20fF, and the power clock frequency is set to 5MHz.

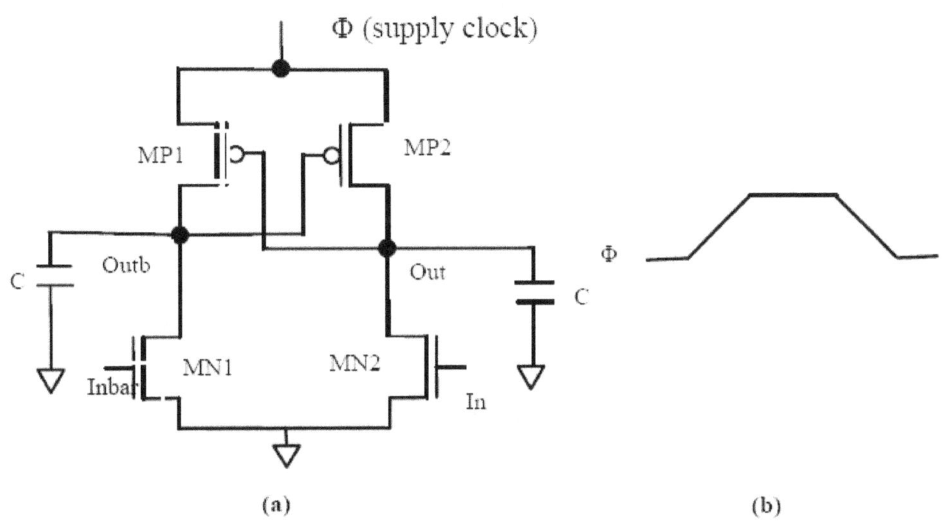

Figure 4.4 ECRL inverter and supply clock [53]

During the first cycle, which lasts from 0 ns to 100 ns, node out remains low and *outb* follows the supply clock. Because the input values have changed, the outputs are reversed in the next cycle from 100 ns to 200 ns. The energy is recovered in energy graph, but not totally when the supply clock decreases. When compared to other logic families, this energy loss is negligible. Because the change of logic value in the previous stage might impact the following stage, ECRL would spend excessive power with two-phase clocking. As a result, four-phase clocking is advised for effective energy savings.

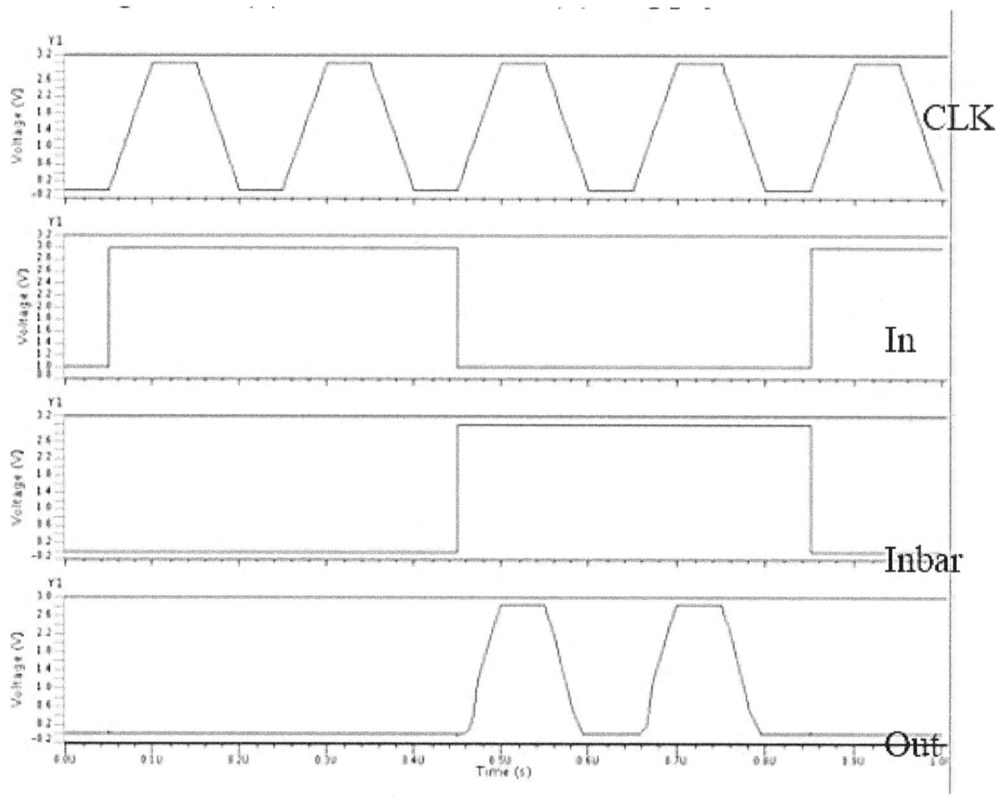

Figure 4.5 ECRL inverter output waveform [53]

4.4.2 Positive Feedback Adiabatic Logic (PFAL)

Positive Feedback Adiabatic Logic (PFAL), a quasi static and differential logic adiabatic family, has been identified as one of the most resilient, with a considerable reduction in power usage. Power Gating has been modified to cut power dissipation even further. It is performed by the use of sleep state control units, which switch circuits between awake and idle states. The concept of adiabatic charge recovery is used in positive feedback adiabatic logic (PFAL). The adiabatic logic describes a situation in which a transition can occur without the use of energy in the form of heat. Low power circuits enable the use of reversible logic to save energy. Figure 4.6 depicts the basic structure of positive feedback adiabatic logic (PFAL).

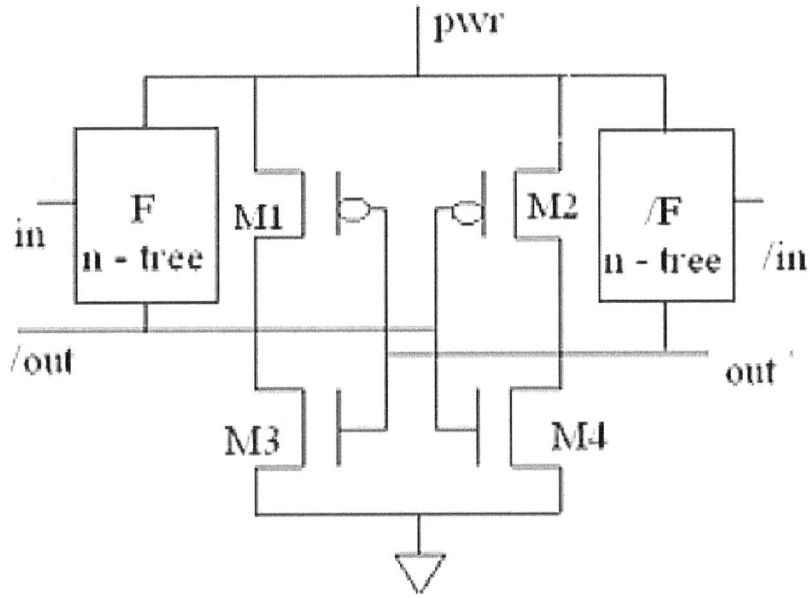

Figure 4.6 Basic structure of positive feedback adiabatic logic [3]

The adiabatic circuits operate on the assumption of the adiabatic charging and discharging process. It is intended for use in a partial energy recovery circuit and has the lowest energy usage when compared to comparable counterparts. It has the highest level of resistance to changes in technical parameters. The basis of all the PFAL gates in this figure is an adiabatic amplifier, which is the latch created with two PMOS (M1 – M2) and two NMOS (M3 – M4), which helps to minimize logic level deterioration on the output nodes out and /out. The logic functions are to be used to realize the two n – trees. The basic structure of Four Phase Trapezoidal Clock was shown in Figure 4.7.

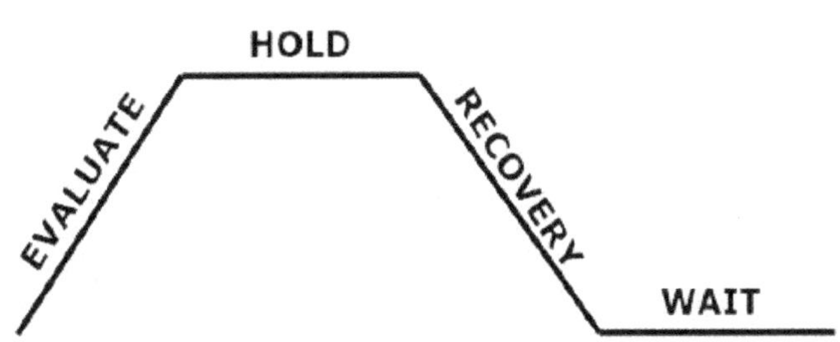

Figure 4.7 Four Phase Trapezoidal Clock [3]

It's the high adaptability to changes in technological parameters. It is a twin rail circuit with some energy recovery. The partial energy recovery circuit construction will employ positive feedback adiabatic logic. When compared to other similar families, this has the lowest energy usage and strong resistance to technical parameters. The PFAL gate is an adiabatic amplifier with a latch created by two PMOS and two NMOS logic gates. This strategy aids in avoiding a significant level of deterioration on the output nodes. Positive and negative outputs will be created by this logic family. This system consists of two cross-coupled inverters and NMOs transistor blocks linked in parallel to the PMOS, which must decrease logic level deterioration on output. This method is based on a positive loop gain with low resistance. There are four phase power clocks to be linked in the adiabatic logic, and charging is done step by step with the assistance of the power supply. The timing diagram will be depicted in the figure 4.8.

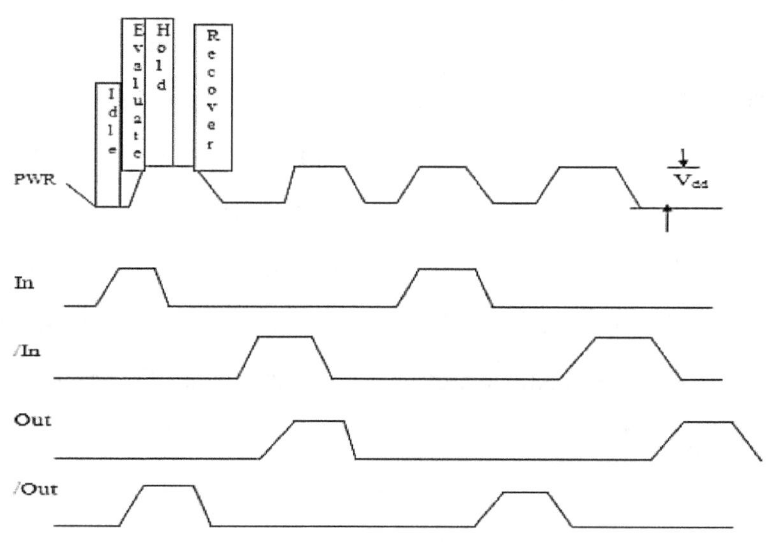

Figure 4.8 Timing diagram of PFAL

This figure will show the oscillating power supply, the dual rail encoded signal (In, /In), and the output signal (Out, /Out). The positive feedback adiabatic logic will be used to generate this timing diagram.

4.4.2.1 Logic design and operation

The PFAL partial energy recovery structure consumes the least amount of energy when compared to other families and has a high level of tolerance to changes in technological parameters. Figure 1 shows the overall design of PFAL (a). It is a dual-rail circuit with some energy recovery. An adiabatic amplifier, a latch composed of two PMOS M1-M2 and two NMOS M3-M4, is at the heart of all PFAL gates, preventing logic level deterioration at output nodes out and /out. The logic function is realized by the two n-trees, which provide complementary output. When charging the capacitance, the functional block is connected in parallel to the PMOSFETs of the adiabatic amplifier to generate transmission gates with low equivalent resistance.

PFAL employs a four-phase system. Assume that input nodes, In is set to high and /In is set to low. When the power clock rises from 0 to Vdd at the start of the cycle, out remains at ground level and power flows via F. (n-tree). When the power clock hits Vdd, the output retains the proper logic. These values are kept throughout the hold phase and used as input to the following stage. After holding stage power clock to 0, /out returns its energy to power clock, allowing deliver charge to be restored.

4.5 GATED HYBRID ENERGY RECOVERY LOGIC (GHERL)

The XOR gate is a key component in the S-Box architecture of the AES algorithm. To achieve strong security against information leakage in terms of power consumption, it should be necessary to concentrate on the design of a fundamental logic gate. Figure 4.9 depicts the schematic diagram of the GHERL XOR gate.

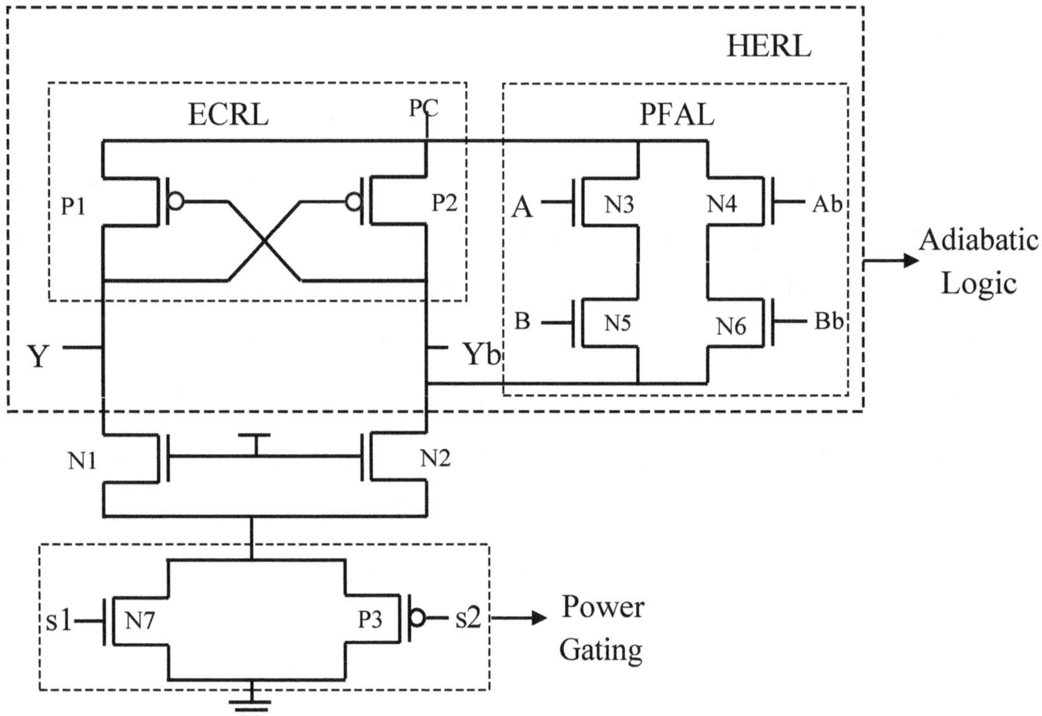

Figure 4.9 GHERL XOR gate

In a single design, it can do both XOR and XNOR operations. This architecture's inputs are A, B, Ab, Bb, S1 and S2. Ab and Bb are A and B's complementary inputs. Y represents the XOR output of A and B, whereas Yb represents the XNOR output of A and B. S1 and S2 are control transistors that operate as sleep transistors.

The power clock that creates the power supply is known as PC, and it has four modes of operation: evaluation, wait, hold, and recovery mode. If both sleep transistors are set to high in recovery mode (PC=1), or if S1='1' and S2='0', it runs in active mode and performs standard XOR operation. It operates in standby mode under the remaining circumstances. PMOS transistors are denoted by P1, P2, and P3, whereas NMOS transistors are denoted by N1, N2, N3, N4, N5, N6, and N7. Because the gate inputs of transistors N1 and N2 are coupled to the supply voltage Vdd, they are constantly conducting. If the suggested design's inputs are similar, the circuit's response is low; if any of the inputs is high, the circuit's output reaction is high.

4.6 POWER CONSUMPTION

The power consumption of a design indicates how much energy is consumed per operation as well as how much heat is dissipated by the circuit. Power dissipation is a significant design feature that influences feasibility, cost, and reliability. The following equation may be used to calculate total power usage.

$$P_{avg} = P_{switching} + P_{short-circuit} + P_{static} \quad (4.1)\ [54]$$

$$P_{avg} = \frac{1}{2}\alpha CLV_{dd}2f + I_{sc}V_{dd} + I_{leakage}V_{dd} \quad (4.2)\ [54]$$

$P_{switching}$ is the dynamic component of power, CL denotes load capacitance, f denotes clock frequency, and is the switching activity. The switching power equation is proportional to the square of the supply voltage (Vdd). The short circuit current Isc caused by the direct channel between the supply rails during output transitions causes $P_{short-circuit}$. P_{static} is caused by the leakage current Ileakage, which is a sum of the bias and sub-threshold currents. The switching power dissipation is the most significant cause of power dissipation. Because switching power is related to the square of the operating voltage, lowering the voltage is the most effective way to reduce power usage.

And now we have created circuits with a low overall transistor count and a low number of transistors functioning at the same time in the circuit. As a result, overall dynamic and static power consumption is lowered. The suggested designs reduce short-circuit power consumption by removing static routes, which are dependent on the rise and fall timings of inputs and outputs. The suggested circuits feature identical input and output edge timings, resulting in minimal short-circuit current flows and power consumption.

4.7 LEAKAGE POWER ANALYSIS

Leakage power is rising dramatically as technology advances, and it is now a significant component to overall chip power dissipation. Together, the three forms of leakages, namely sub-threshold leakage, gate leakage, and reverse bias junction band-to-band tunneling leakage currents, account for more than 25% of power consumption in today's leading-edge systems. Different leakage sources might interact with one another via the intermediate node voltages that occur. This is known as the loading effect, and it causes an increase in leakage current. Sub-threshold leakage current, on the other hand, diminishes as the number of transistors stacked in series increases. This is known as the stack effect. Because the leakage power consumption of a gate depends on the input vector state at the gate, the overall leakage power consumption of a circuit is input-pattern dependent, i. e., the value varies as the input signal to the circuit changes.

The reliance of leakage on process fluctuations is greater than the dependency on input vector states. As a result, evaluating the variance of average leakage current for all potential input patterns to the circuit is adequate to anticipate the impact of process variations on total circuit leakage. However, estimating the average leakage by simulating the circuit at all input patterns is impracticable, thus an input pattern-independent technique is preferable. Probabilistic approaches have been employed in switching power estimates. A similar technique in which the average leakage current of each gate is computed and the overall average circuit leakage is estimated as the sum of the average leakage currents of all gates:

$$I_{tot}^{avg} = \sum_{k=1}^{N_g} I_{leak,k}^{avg} \tag{4.3}$$

$$I_{tot}^{avg} = \sum_{k=1}^{N_g} \sum_{\forall vec_{i,k}} prob(vec_{i,k}).I_{leak,k}(vec_{i,k}) \tag{4.4}$$

where N_g is the total number of gates in the circuit, $I_{leak,k}^{avg}$ is the average leakage current of the k th gate, $vec_{i,k}$is the I th input vector at the k th gate, $prob(vec_{i,k})$ is the probability of occurrence of $vec_{i,k}$and $I_{leak,k}(vec_{i,k})$ is the leakage current of the k th gate. The probability distribution of the average circuit leakage current I_{tot}^{avg} as expressed in Equation 4.4. Under process fluctuations, taking into consideration both sub threshold and gate tunneling leakage currents. The leakage current is largely reliant on the steady-state terminal voltage of the transistor, which is governed by the CMOS circuit's logic state as determined by the input pattern. As a result, there is a pattern that produces the greatest leakage current. This study takes into account all leakage sources and attempts to discover an input pattern(s) that will maximize the composite leakage current composed of all components.

4.8 RESULTS AND DISCUSSION

The proposed GHERL XOR gate based S-Box is designed and simulated using Tanner EDA with 125 nm technology. The performances of the proposed S-Box and GHERL XOR gate are analyzed in terms of area, delay, power consumption, and energy consumption.

4.8.1 Performance Evaluation of Proposed GHERL XOR Gate

The area of HERL XOR gate with power gating techniques is measured by transistor count and it is shown in Figure 4.10. Power gating is a method used in integrated circuit design to decrease power consumption by turning off the current to non-utilized circuit blocks. Power gating offers the added benefit of enabling Iddq testing in addition to minimizing stand-by or leakage power. Power gating has a greater impact on design architecture than clock gating. It lengthens time delays since power gated modes must be entered and left securely. There are architectural trade-offs between designing for the amount of leakage power savings in low power modes and the energy dissipation required to enter and exit low power modes.

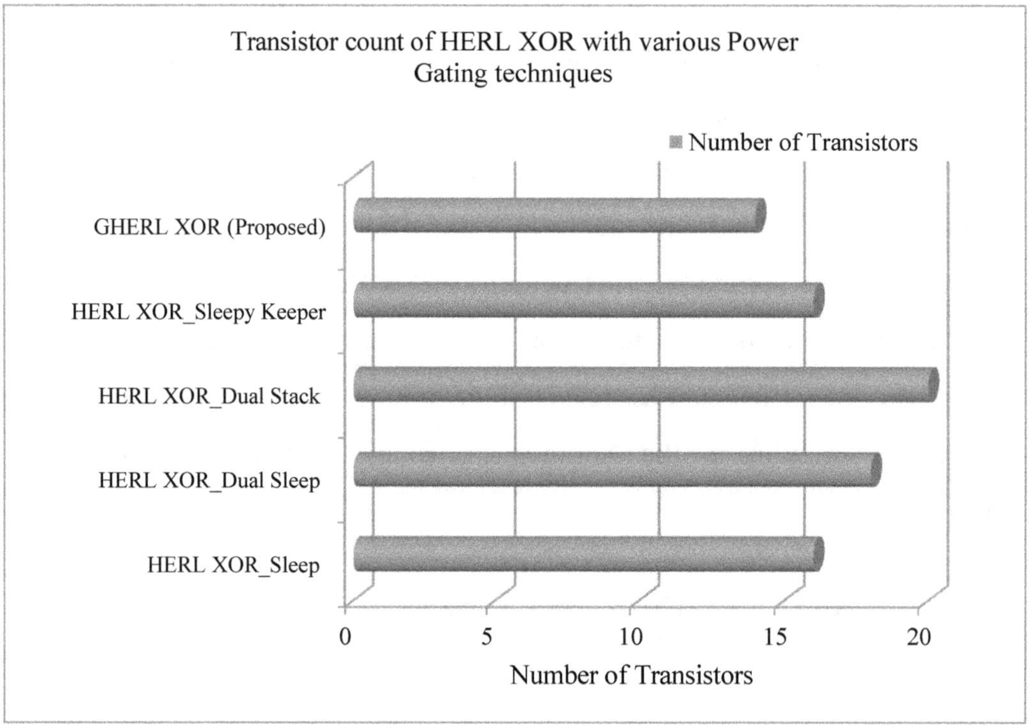

Figure 4.10 Area Analysis of HERL XOR

An externally switched power supply is a very simple type of power gating used to reduce long-term leaking power. Internal power gating is more appropriate for turning off the block for short periods of time. Power gating controllers regulate the CMOS switches that supply power to the circuitry. The power gated block's outputs discharge slowly. As a result, output voltage levels spend more time at the threshold voltage level. This might result in a higher short circuit current. Power gating employs low-leakage PMOS transistors as header switches to turn off power supply to components of a design that are in standby or sleep mode. Sleep transistors may also be made using NMOS footer switches. Inserting the sleep transistors divides the chip's power network into two parts: a permanent power network that is connected to the power source and a virtual power network that drives the cells and may be switched off.

The utilization of fewer transistors in the design also leads to low power consumption. So it is necessary to focus on the transistors count to reduce the power consumption as well as to achieve high security. The comparison graph shows that the proposed GHERL XOR gate reduces the number of transistors by 12.5%, 22.22%, 30%, and 12.5% when compared with HERL XOR with sleep transistor, dual sleep, dual-stack and sleepy keeper approach.

4.8.2 Power and Energy Consumption of Proposed GHERL XOR Gate

The energy consumed by HERL XOR gate with various power gating techniques is measured in atto joules (1 atto $=10^{-18}$) and it is tabulated in Table 4.1. The proposed GHERL XOR gate reduces the power consumption and energy consumption by 74.24%, 63.41%, 44.91%, 13.04% and 87.34%, 26.60%, 3.61%, 13.97% when compared with HERL XOR with sleep, dual sleep, dual-stack and sleepy keeper approach.

The graphical representation of power and energy consumption of HERL XOR with power gating technique was shown in Figure 4.11. The Power Consumption and Energy Consumption of HERL XOR with Sleep Transistor, HERL XOR with Dual Sleep, HERL XOR with Dual Stack, HERL XOR with Sleepy Approach and GHERL XOR are shown in this graph.

Table 4.1 Power and energy consumption of HERL XOR with power gating techniques

Technique	Power Consumption (µW)	Energy Consumption (aJ)
HERL XOR with Sleep Transistor	0.233	0.632
HERL XOR with Dual Sleep	0.164	0.109
HERL XOR with Dual Stack	0.109	0.083
HERL XOR with Sleepy Approach	0.069	0.093
GHERL XOR	0.060	0.080

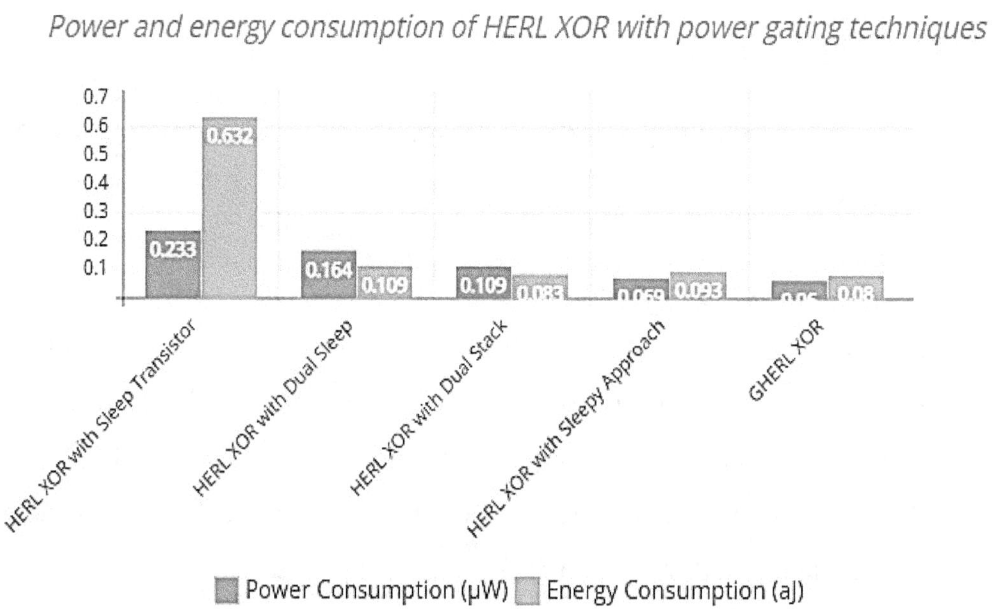

Figure 4.11 Graphical representation of power and energy consumption of HERL XOR

In this Figure 4.11, the power consumption of each technique is represented using blue colour and energy consumption of each technique is represented using green colour.

4.8.3 Leakage Power of Proposed GHERL XOR Gate

Leakage power is defined as the power used by sub-threshold currents and reverse biased diodes in a CMOS transistor. Because the leakage power of a CMOS logic gate is independent of the input transition or load capacitance, it remains constant for a logic cell. The current that goes through the protected ground conductor to ground is referred to as leakage current. It is the current that might flow from any conductive component or the surface of a non-conductive part to ground if a conductive channel was provided in the absence of a grounding connection. Extraneous currents are always flowing in the safety ground conductor. Leakage power of HERL XOR gate with various power gating techniques are shown in Figure 4.12.

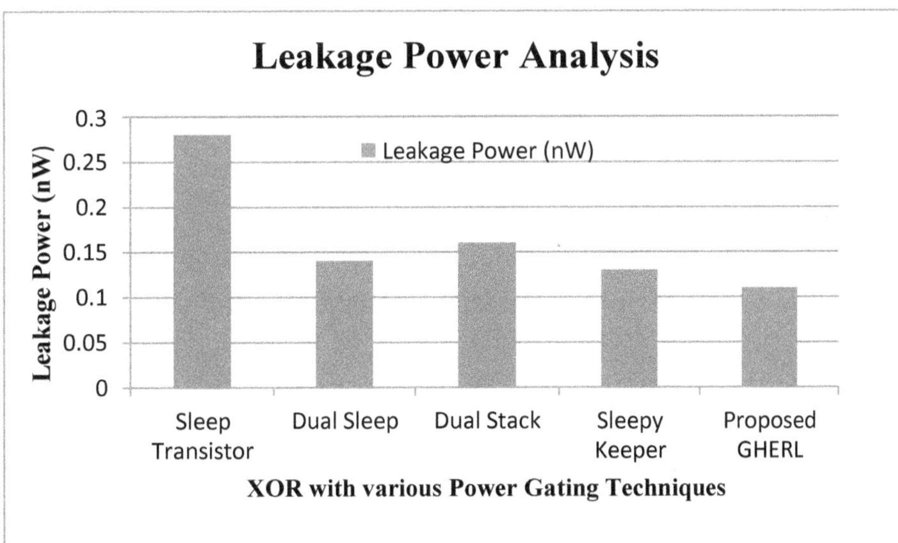

Figure 4.12 Leakage power of XOR with power gating techniques

From the above comparison graph, it is observed that the proposed GHERL XOR gate reduces the leakage power by 58.54%, 20.27%, 27.38% and 13.63% when compared with HERL XOR with power gating techniques such as sleep transistor, dual sleep, dual stack and sleepy keeper approach.

4.8.4 Evaluation of Resistance against Power Analysis Attacks

The resilience to power analysis assaults may be quantified using Normalized Energy Deviation (NED) and Normalized Standard Deviation (NSD). NED is defined as the ratio of the difference between maximum and minimum energy consumption to maximum energy consumption for all conceivable input combinations. NSD calculates the variance in energy consumption due to changes in inputs. If both of these parameters provide a value of zero, it suggests that the system is more resistant to power analysis assaults. The following formulae can be used to calculate NED and NSD.

$$\mathrm{NED} = \frac{e_{max} - e_{min}}{e_{max}} \quad (4.5)$$

Where e_{max} denotes maximum energy consumption and e_{min} denotes minimum energy consumption.

$$\mathrm{NSD} = \frac{\sigma_e}{e_{max} - e_{min}} \quad (4.6)$$

Where σ_e denotes the standard deviation of the energy dissipated by the circuit.

To demonstrate the resistance efficiency of the proposed GHERL XOR gate, the values of NED and NSD are computed for the Symmetric Adiabatic Logic (SyAL) based XOR, Charge Sharing Symmetric Adiabatic Logic (CSSAL) based XOR gate, and Proposed GHERL XOR gate. The NED and NSD are calculated by altering the operating frequencies, and the results are given in Table 4.2.

Table 4.2 NED and NSD of various adiabatic logic XOR gates

Operating Frequency (MHz)	Normalized Energy Deviation			Normalized Standard Deviation		
	SyAL [17]	CSSAL [18]	GHERL	SyAL	CSSAL	GHERL
1	0.020	0.018	0.011	0.040	0.030	0.025
1.5	0.014	0.013	0.009	0.035	0.028	0.019
2	0.012	0.011	0.007	0.031	0.025	0.015
3	0.011	0.008	0.003	0.028	0.022	0.012

The normalized energy deviation of various adiabatic logic XOR gates are represented in figure4.13. The values are taken from table 4.2.

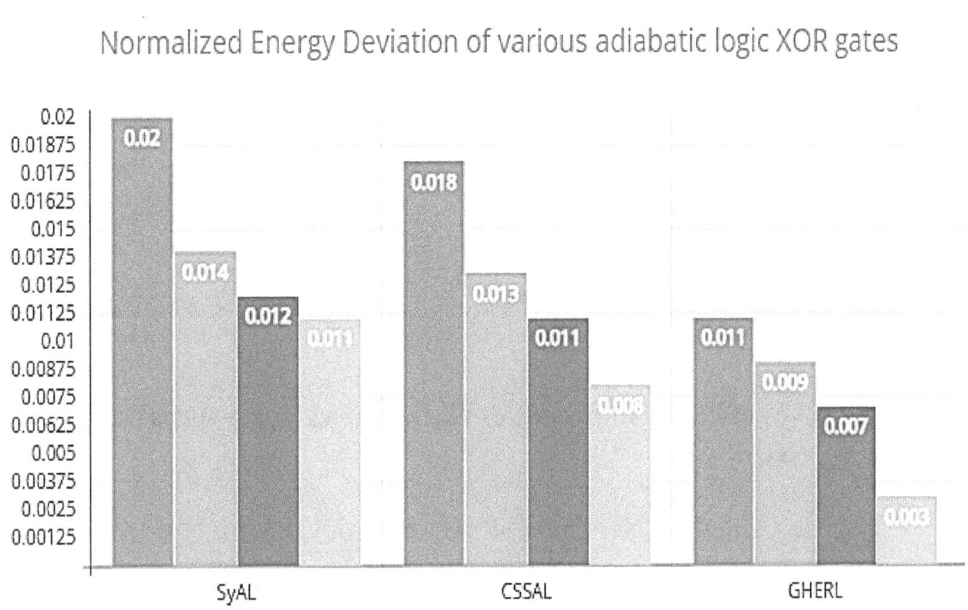

Figure 4.13 Normalized energy deviation of varies adiabatic logic XOR gates

The values of Normalized energy deviation (NED) is computed for the Symmetric Adiabatic Logic (SyAL) based XOR, Charge Sharing Symmetric Adiabatic Logic (CSSAL) based XOR gate, and Proposed GHERL XOR gate which represented in the above graph. The Normalized energy deviation (NED) of SyAL, CSSAL and GHERL at Operating Frequency of 1MHz, 1.5 MHz, 2 MHz, and 3MHz are represented in blue, green, purple and yellow color respectively.

The normalized standard deviation of varies adiabatic logic XOR gates are represented in figure4.14. The values are taken from table 4.2.

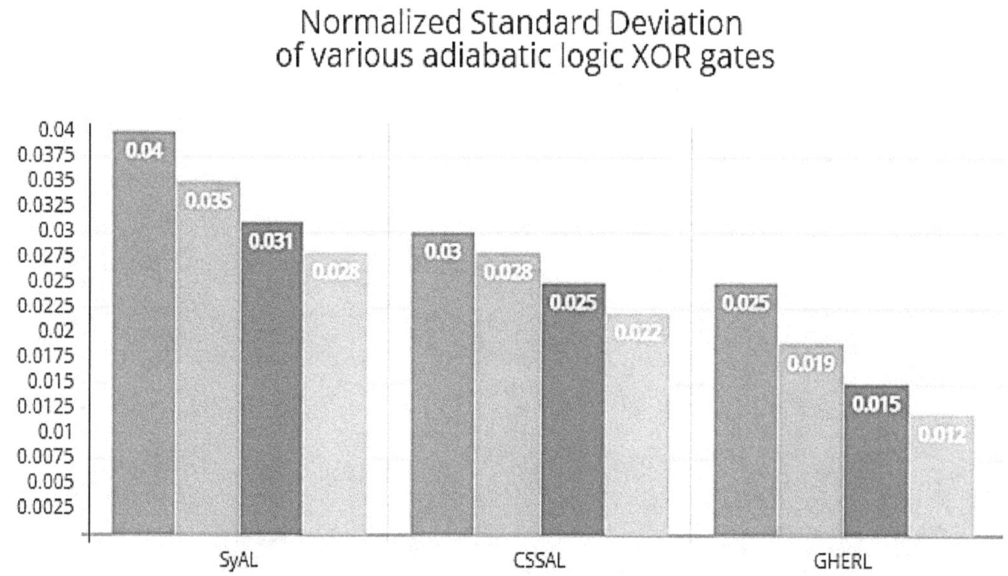

Figure 4.14 Normalized standard deviation of varies adiabatic logic XOR gates

The values of Normalized standard deviation (NED) are obtained for the Symmetric Adiabatic Logic (SyAL) based XOR gate, Charge Sharing Symmetric Adiabatic Logic (CSSAL) based XOR gate, and Proposed GHERL XOR gate shown in the graph above. The normalized energy deviation (NED) of SyAL, CSSAL, and GHERL at 1MHz, 1.5MHz, 2MHz, and 3MHz operating frequencies are displayed in blue, green, purple, and yellow, respectively.

From the tabulated results, it is observed that the GHERL reduces the NED by 45%, 35.71%, 41.66%, 27.27% and 38.88%, 30.76%, 36.36%, 62.5% for 1 MHz, 1.5 MHz, 2 MHz, 3MHZ when compared with SyAL and CSSAL. The proposed GHERL saves NSD by 57.14% and 45.45% for 3MHz when compared with the existing techniques such as SyAL and CSSAL.

4.9 SUMMARY

IoT network is an interconnection of the smart devices that need to maintain high security, high energy efficiency, and low power consumption. The conventional AES is not applicable for high-security applications due to the information leakage. To mitigate this issue, AES is designed using GHERL XOR gate that is a combination of adiabatic logic and power gating. Both are power reduction techniques that reduce the power consumption by recovery logic and shut off the current flow to the blocks that are not in use. The proposed GHERL XOR gate reduces the power consumption and energy consumption by 74.24%, 63.41%, 44.91%, 13.04% and 87.34%, 26.60%, 3.61%, 13.97% when compared with HERL XOR with sleep, dual sleep, dual-stack and sleepy keeper approach.

CHAPTER 5

S-BOX DESIGNS

5.1 INTRODUCTION

The Advanced Encryption Standard (AES) has recently been introduced to address the shortcomings of prior symmetric-key cryptography systems such as DES and 3DES. The AES, in particular, has remedied the shortcomings of prior standards in terms of brute-force attack vulnerability and slow software implementation. As a result, the AES has been used in a variety of security-constrained applications since its approval as the symmetric-key standard in 2001. The transmitter and receiver of sensitive data exchange a secret key to maintain the information's confidentiality while using AES. Despite this, a malicious attacker might gain access to the secret key and compromise the standard. One way for retrieving side-channel information is fault attacks, for which numerous methodologies have been proposed.

In the redundant unit fault detection approach, the strategies are described. It should be highlighted that such a results in 100% overheads in terms of area, power, and latency. In addition, the technique suggests detecting temporary flaws by repeating the modifications in an AES cycle for the same input. The method proposes new S-box and inverse S-box structures with higher complexities than that of the original structures for detecting 100 percent of single faults. The merging S-box (SB) and inverse S-box (ISB) are used to suggest a concurrent fault detection system. It should also be highlighted that the offered strategies take into account the entire search space of composite fields in order to present the best lightweight defect detection schemes.

Furthermore, the strategy is dependent on the AES's implementation of functional redundancy. The scheme given is applicable to all transformations in AES encryption and decryption, regardless of how they are implemented. It should also be highlighted that the proposed approach employs double-data-rate computing to mitigate fault attacks. A fault detection system based on Hamming and Reed-Solomon codes is also presented in protecting the storage elements inside the AES. Only the S-box and the inverse S-box are nonlinear among the AES' four distinct transformations. Furthermore, all S-boxes (and their inverse S-boxes) take up a large portion of the whole AES encryption (and decryption) area, and their power consumption is around three-quarters of that of the complete AES. The AES S-boxes and inverse S-boxes can be implemented in hardware using LUTs. However, this implementation is not suited for applications that require AES implementations that are fast and low-complexity.

As a result, it is emphasized on low-area implementations of S-boxes and inverse S-boxes with composite fields in this study. This approach has received a lot of attention in the literature. Low-power implementations of the S-boxes (and their inverse S-boxes) exist as well, such as the ones described here. It should be noted that the presented low-power S-box employs composite fields.

An S-box must meet specific design characteristics in order to be resistant to cryptanalysis assaults of various types. The bit-wise functional non – linearity (NL) and linear approximation probability (LAP) tests are two of the criteria used to establish S-box resistance to linear cryptanalysis. Many 90 iphers require S-boxes with high non-linearity since they are the only nonlinear component. S-box building is difficult for ciphers that rely on secret key-dependent dynamic S-boxes. To begin with, pseudorandom S-box designs have an unacceptable non-linearity distribution. As a result, S-boxes must be meticulously built to provide high non-linearity. Second, the dynamic S-box must be modified regularly with each session, message, or even message block to prevent adversaries from getting enough information to deduce the encryption key. In real-time applications, this need imposes strict limits on the S-box building pace. Finally, there should be a large enough number of alternative S-boxes to prevent brute-force guessing of the secret S-box.

The S-Box design criteria decide whether or not an S-Box is suitable for a certain cryptographic application. Bijectivity, nonlinearity, linear approximation probability, differential approximation probability, input-output tight avalanche criterion, and output-bit independence criterion are some of the requirements.

To design an S-box, It is utilized an algebraic property of linear fractional transformation and its application on $GF(2^n)$ where n = 8 having elements from 0 to 255. By using the properties of$GF(2^8)$, the produced S-box will be composed of 256-bit of elements. The proposed S-box is made using the linear fractional transformation and permutation function techniques. The purpose of adding a permutation function is to improve this S-non-linear box's features. As a result, before and after the permutation function is applied, a security analysis of the S-box is performed to see how effective the permutation function is at increasing S-box security.

5.2 S-BOX DESIGN USING HERL LOGIC

S-Box is a displacement component that is used in symmetric cryptographic methods. It is the first step in AES encryption, followed by byte substitution, shifting rows, mixing columns, and adding a round key. S-Box design using proposed HERL logic is shown in Figure 5.1.

S-Box is represented in this study by a Galois Field (GF), which is also known as a Finite Field because it has a finite number of elements. Isomorphic mapping is a type of mapping that decomposes higher-order fields into lower-order fields. The first step in S-Box design is isomorphic mapping, which reduces the design's complexity. For isomorphic mapping, the 8-bit input is used. The isomorphic mapping's output is separated into 4 higher-order bits and 4 lower-order bits.

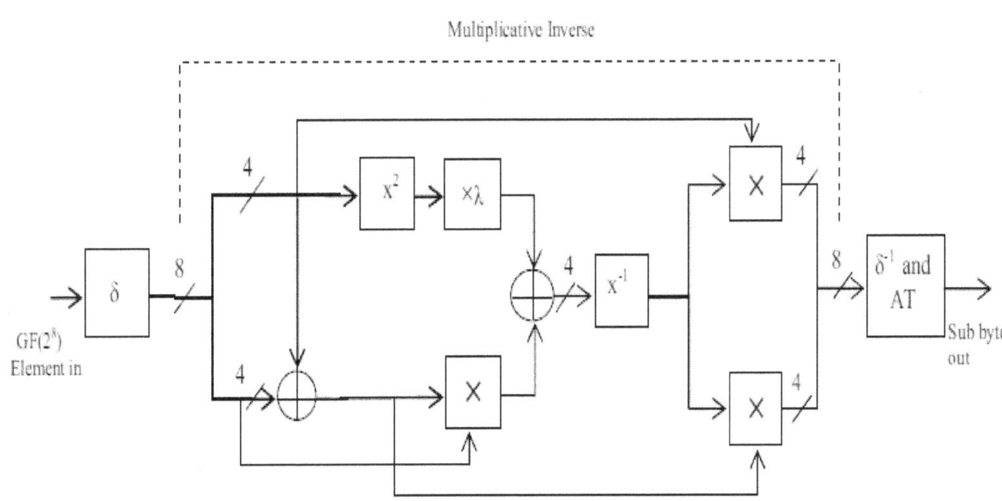

Figure 5.1 Proposed S-Box Design with HERL logic

The squarer receives the higher-order bits as input, and then performs an XOR operation on the higher-order and lower-order bits. The squarer receives the higher-order bits as input, and then performs an XOR operation on the higher-order and lower-order bits. The result of multiplying the squarer's answer by a constant λ is applied to the XOR gate, which performs an XOR operation with the product obtained by multiplying the lower order bits by the preceding result. Then Multiplicative Inverse is applied and pre-computed results are shown in Table 5.1.

Table 5.1 Pre-computed Results from Multiplicative Inverse

m	0	1	2	3	4	5	6	7	8	9	A	B	C	D	E	F
m^{-1}	0	1	3	2	F	C	9	B	A	6	8	7	5	E	D	4

It can be computed by the following equations

$$m_3^{-1} = m_3 \oplus m_3 m_2 m_1 \oplus m_3 m_0 \oplus m_2 \tag{5.1}$$

$$m_2^{-1} = m_3 m_2 m_1 \oplus m_3 m_2 m_0 \oplus m_3 m_0 \oplus m_2 \oplus m_2 m_1 \tag{5.2}$$

$$m_1^{-1} = m_3 \oplus m_3 m_2 m_1 \oplus m_3 m_1 m_0 \oplus m_2 \oplus m_2 m_0 \oplus m_1 \tag{5.3}$$

$$m_0^{-1} = m_3 m_2 m_1 \oplus m_3 m_2 m_0 \oplus m_3 m_1 \oplus m_3 m_1 m_0 \oplus m_3 m_0 \oplus m_2 \oplus m_2 m_1 m_0 \oplus m_1 \oplus m_0 \tag{5.4}$$

The multiplicative inverse's response is applied to the GF (24) multiplier, which may be obtained using the GF (22) multiplier. GF (22) is implemented using GF (2) to simplify the complexity of the design. The 4-bit multiplier outputs are concatenated, and then converted to the composite field via an isomorphic inverse operation, and lastly the byte substitution output is achieved.

An S-box built using a certain technique may be a weak S-box, making it an easy target for invaders. A powerful S-box has the ability to withstand such assaults and secure data. Although the S-box-based picture encryption approach is simulated for gray-scale photos, it may simply be scaled to encrypt colour images as well.

5.3 S-BOX DESIGN USING HERL AND GHERL BASED XOR GATE

The operation of S-Box design using HERL based XOR gate is same as the S-Box design using GHERL based XOR gate. This proposed S-Box is specially designed for byte substitution process which is an initial process of AES. Among the four operations in AES, sub bytes is non linear function and the remaining shift rows, mix columns and add round key are linear function. The architecture of proposed S-Box design is shown in Figure 3. The XOR gate used in the proposed structure denotes HERL XOR or GHERL XOR.

The proposed S-Box design accepts the input as 8-bit and generates the output as 8-bit. Here Galois Field (GF) termed as finite field is preferred by the researcher to represent both the inputs and outputs. The major operations of the proposed S-Box design are Isomorphic mapping to the composite field, (δ), Squarer (x2), multiplication with constant (xλ), multiplicative inversion (x-1), multiplication, Inverse isomorphic mapping (δ-1) and Affine Transformation (AT).

It can generate 16x16 matrixes LUT by performing the substitution and permutation. Let the 8-bit input to the S-Box design is I, then the mapping process can be computed by the following mathematical expression

$$j = (\delta \times i) = \begin{bmatrix} i_7 \oplus i_5 \\ i_7 \oplus i_6 \oplus i_4 \oplus i_3 \oplus i_2 \oplus i_1 \\ i_7 \oplus i_5 \oplus i_3 \oplus i_2 \\ i_7 \oplus i_5 \oplus i_3 \oplus i_2 \oplus i_1 \\ i_7 \oplus i_6 \oplus i_2 \oplus i_1 \\ i_7 \oplus i_4 \oplus i_3 \oplus i_2 \oplus i_1 \\ i_6 \oplus i_4 \oplus i_1 \\ i_6 \oplus i_1 \oplus i_0 \end{bmatrix} \quad (5.5)$$

Here, the XOR operator $\oplus$represents HERL/ GHERL XOR gate. The response obtained from the δ block is categorized into higher order 4 bits and lower order 4 bits. The higher order 4 bits are accepted by the squarer block and it performs the following operations.

$$K_3 = j_{h3} \quad (5.6)$$

$$k_2 = j_{h3} \oplus j_{h2} \quad (5.7)$$

$$k_1 = j_{h2} \oplus j_{h1} \quad (5.8)$$

$$k_0 = j_{h3} \oplus j_{h1} \oplus j_{h0} \quad (5.9)$$

The output obtained from the squarer block is multiplied with the parameter λ to denote it in GF format and can be expressed by the following expressions

$$l_3 = k_2 \oplus k_0 \quad (5.10)$$

$$l_2 = k_3 \oplus k_2 \oplus k_1 \oplus k_0 \quad (5.11)$$

$$l_1 = k_3 \quad (5.12)$$

$$l_0 = k_2 \quad (5.13)$$

$GF(2^4)$ multiplier accepts the inputs as XOR value (m) of lower order bits with higher order bits and lower order 4 bits. It is a combination of GF (2^2) multipliers and it can be expressed by the following mathematical expressions.

$$N_1 = j_{l1}m_1 \oplus j_{l0}m_1 \oplus j_{l1}m_0 \quad (5.14)$$

$$n_0 = j_{l1}m_1 \oplus j_{l0}m_0 \quad (5.15)$$

The output from the GF (2^4) multiplier is denoted by p. XOR operation is performed between p and l and the response from the XOR block is mentioned as q. Then multiplicative inverse is applied to q that can be computed by the following equations

$$q_3^{-1} = q_3 \oplus q_3 q_2 q_1 \oplus q_3 q_0 \oplus q_2 \quad (5.16)$$

$$q_2^{-1} = q_3 q_2 q_1 \oplus q_3 q_2 q_0 \oplus q_3 q_0 \oplus q_2 \oplus q_2 q_1 \quad (5.17)$$

$$q_1^{-1} = q_3 \oplus q_3 q_2 q_1 \oplus q_3 q_1 q_0 \oplus q_2 \oplus q_2 q_0 \oplus q_1 \quad (5.18)$$

$$q_o^{-1} = q_3 q_2 q_1 \oplus q_3 q_2 q_0 \oplus q_3 q_1 \oplus q_3 q_1 q_0 \oplus q_3 q_0 \oplus q_2 \oplus q_2 q_1 \oplus q_2 q_1 q_0 \oplus q_1 \oplus q_0 \quad (5.19)$$

Then GF (2^4) multiplication is done between the response from the multiplicative inverse and higher-order lower-order bits from the δ block. The response from the GF (2^4) multipliers are concatenated and then given to the δ^{-1} block to generate the sub byte output. The XOR gate plays a vital role in every function of the S-Box design. So the GHERL XOR gate is proposed in cryptography applications with low power dissipation to reduce the leakage information and to achieve high security.

5.4 CIPHER

A cipher that uses static S-boxes in its operations does not provide adequate data protection since attackers may gain information of such S-boxes through some means and create plaintext as a result. Invaders attempted assaults against ciphers like Data Encryption Standard (DES) and Advanced Encryption Standard (AES) by exploiting the feebleness of the related S-boxes. To compensate for the shortcomings and fragility of static S-boxes, modern cryptographic algorithms use dynamic S-boxes in their operations to profit from the cryptographic strengths associated with these S-boxes.

The cryptographic strength of the generated S-box and other rampant S-boxes found in the literature is assessed using a conventional S-box criterion. The proposed plan for the installation of dynamic and strong S-boxes makes an important contribution, according to comparative performance study. The proposed S-box is also used to illustrate its suitability for multimedia data encryption by presenting a fast and efficient image protection solution with high throughput.

The cryptographic strength of the generated S-box and other massive S-boxes available in the literature is assessed using a standard S-box criterion. The proposed plan for the installation of dynamic and strong S-boxes makes a significant contribution, according to comparative performance study.

An S-box plays an imperative role in producing a non-linear connection among plaintext and cipher text by inciting added muddle for the attackers of captured data from insecure communication channels. It is the solitary non-linear constituent of a block cipher and has the capability to engender more jumbles in the resultant cipher text for the invaders as compared to other constituents of the respective block cipher that work linearly and contribute less in the protection. Consequently, the protection of plaintext provided by a block cipher that employs S-box in its structure against attacks is directly reliant on the cryptographic forte of the respective S-box. S-boxes employed in the working of a cipher are referred as static and dynamic one An S-box having a constant place for each random value always is known as a static S-box.

The S-box has been demonstrated to be the cornerstone of modern symmetric ciphers such as block and stream ciphers, as well as a key component in any block system layout. However, cryptanalysis can exploit some flaws in the S-box render. In any block cipher system, the S-box is also a crucial phase. A fixed or a static S-box, which means the same S-box will be used in every round, are the two sorts of S-boxes. A fixed S-box allows attackers to examine the S-attributes Box's and pinpoint its weak places. The elements of the fixed structure of S-boxes are the major challenge in developing any block cipher scheme. The S-boxes in the Data Encryption Standard algorithm are an example of a fixed S-box.

In the form of a Linear Approximation Table (LAT) or Walsh transform and Difference Distribution Table (DDT) or autocorrelation table and spectrum, S-boxes can be analyzed using linear and differential cryptanalysis. The nonlinearity (bent, almost bent) and differential uniformity can be used to summarize its strength.

An S-box contributes significantly to the meaninglessness of plaintext prior to transmission, resulting in more jumbles in the invaders' cipher text. As a result, scholars and researchers are looking to determine novel transformations that aid inside the construction of strong S-boxes. We propose a simple and original technique to erect dynamic and durable S-boxes with noteworthy cryptographic power by presenting an innovative and dynamic linear trigonometric transformation and a distinctive heuristic evolution plan.

An S-box has a good quality when it is resistant to linear and differential attacks. This section explains how to make a good S-box and how to test the finished S-boxes.

These steps are:

1. Using the 3 best irreducible polynomials.
2. Forming a new affine matrix using a modified AES S-box affine matrix.
3. Apply an additional 8-bit constant from the AES S-box.

5.5 KEY-DEPENDENT S-BOX

The key-dependent S-box indicates that the S-box changes in every round based on the key and the number of rounds, whereas the static S-box means that the S-box remains the same every round. Attackers can study fixed S-boxes and locate weak places, whereas key-dependent S-boxes make it more difficult for attackers to undertake any offline analysis of an attack on a specific collection of S-boxes. Overall performance in terms of security and speed, on the other hand, has not been adequately addressed or thoroughly studied.

5.6 GALOIS FIELD

As is the case with the AES, S-boxes are frequently constructed as an affine transformation made of an inverse power mapping over some Galois field. This particular power mapping offers a number of desirable cryptographic features that render many known cryptanalysis methods ineffective in practice.

For byte substitution, the S-box is a frequent component of block ciphers. It's a nonlinear function that multiplies the Galois field (GF) before applying an affine transformation. With a transformation into the composite field GF, this algorithm is more efficient. Due to the presence of fast and slow pathways, our prior design advocated a two-stage approach by adding flip-flops to limit glitch power. Due to a longer clock-cycle, we replace the middle flip-flops with latches, allowing this block to have a 1 cycle delay while also saving some space.

Because of the major constraint between classical cryptanalysis and cryptographic features, the creation and design of S-boxes has gotten a lot of attention. Transparency order has also been described in order to quantify S-box DPA robustness. Simulated annealing, a type of metaheuristic search, has emerged as a potentially powerful approach for designing such vectorial Boolean functions. Kirkpatrick developed simulated annealing as either a revolutionary search strategy in 1983, combining hill-climbing with probabilistic acceptance of non-improving moves.

As a result of probabilistic rejection, such local search method eliminates optimal solution. A search space is made up of bijective S-boxes over GF (2n), and the one with good cryptography qualities like high nonlinearity and a low GAC absolute indicator value is expected. Every S-box in the search space represents a potential solution. The search begins with such a unique S-box as an initial state, and then a move is created in the immediate neighborhood. Each step has an objective functions that must be lowered with each subsequent move. The better moves are always accepted, while the bad moves are acknowledged with a probability that is dependent on the search temp T. A handful of motions are evaluated for each value of T.

The temperature T is high at first, and every worsening movement is accepted with a high degree of probability. T cools down as the convergence rate increases, and accepting worsening moves becomes more difficult. Finally, the system comes to a halt, and only better moves are permitted. If after convinced iterations, no improving moves are establish the system halts.

5.7 S-BOX ANALYSIS

S-box is a key component of the secure data transmission procedure over the internet. The findings of numerous modifications, such as a combination of an irreducible polynomial and an affine matrix, are used in the suggested S- box. The three best intrinsic polynomials based on past research are used to modify irreducible polynomials. For each linear matrix member of the AES S-box, the Boolean operation XOR is being used to transform the quadratic matrix. Several elevated S-boxes are made from the combined result of the adjustments.

Non – linearity, stringent avalanche criterion, bit independence criterion-nonlinearity, and bit independence criterion-strict avalanche criterion testing were used to find the optimal S-box quality. The best quality S-box has non – linearity, stringent avalanche criteria, bit independence set of criteria, and bit independence criterion-strict avalanche criterion scores of 112, 0.5015, 112, and 0.4997, respectively. The S-box value can be calculated to use the test findings and a preset statistical procedure. The S-box value in this study is 16.0017, according to the calculations. This shows that the proposed S-box is of higher quality than those created in prior studies.

In iterative block ciphers, S-boxes, also termed as vectorial Boolean functions, play a major role. These block ciphers have many round functions that are made up of S-boxes that are coupled in various ways with the secret key, and the cipher is built by iterating a set number of rounds. A map f0; 1gn! F0; 1gm is a (n;m)-S-box. The coordinate functions of F are the Boolean functions f1;:::;fm established for every x 2 f0; 1gn by F(x) = (f1(x);:::; fm(x)) for a given function F. From literature, cryptanalytic attacks on the block ciphers have imposed several restrictions on the design principles of S-box.

The output derivatives of the S-boxes should be as evenly balanced as way to prevent differential attacks proposed by Biham and Shamir. To resist linear cryptanalysis, the S-nonlinearity boxes should be as high as possible. High algebraic degree, high order correlation immunity, low differential uniformity, and low absolute indicator value of Global Avalanche Characteristics (GAC) are some important cryptographic aspects to consider in S-box design. Because all of these characteristics cannot be addressed simultaneously, S-box design strategies focus on achieving a good trade-off between them.

To achieve the characteristics of compact area, the S-box is primarily constructed using dual premise and the circuit is optimized using an AND-XOR array structure. The S-Box proposed in this research has a smaller area than prior S-Boxes, which is 17.76 percent lower than the actual S-Box. The S-Box is 29.87 percent and 25.34 cents smaller than the polynomial and normal basis, respectively, when compared to other bases.

During the optimization phase, the S-box is tuned to maximize nonlinearity by optimizing the location optimization technique from every employed and unemployed bee. When compared to various state-of-the-art approaches, the experimental outcomes and performance analyses reveal that it can attain higher non – linearity and cryptographic features.

The parameters of dynamic S-Box are similar to those of the standard AES algorithm. Static Box allows attackers to examine S-Box and find flaws, whereas dynamic S-Box makes it tougher and so more complex for attackers to undertake any offline analysis of an attack on a single set of S-boxes. Both methods are implemented in MATLAB, and data gathering input and output are still in hexadecimal format. The suggested AES is compared to the standard AES in terms of security analysis using the avalanche effect test, as simulation times are contrasted between the two algorithms.

5.8 PERFORMANCE OF CRYPTANALYSIS

A specimen S-box is replicated, and established performance criteria are used to compare the cryptographic strength of the resultant S-box to that of other known S-boxes in the literature. Comparative performance analyses show that the suggested technique makes a significant contribution to the production of dynamic and secure S-boxes. To demonstrate that the proposed S-box is a strong candidate for modern cryptograms to protect multimedia data, an image privacy-preserving solution based on this is also proposed.

The S-box has been demonstrated to be the cornerstone of modern symmetric ciphers such as block and stream ciphers, as well as a vital component of any block system layout. Cryptanalysis can expose various flaws in the S-box render. In any block cipher scheme, the S-box is a critical moment. A fixed or a static S-box, which means the same S-box will be used in each round, are the two varieties of S-boxes available. With a fixed S-box, attackers can investigate the S-attributes Box's and find its weak spots. The elements of fixed structure of S-boxes are the major challenge in every encryption algorithm system's implementation. S-boxes in Data Encryption Standard algorithm are an example of a fixed S-box.

The basis of such DES-like cryptosystems is an S-box that gives these cryptosystems the confusion property proposed by Shannon in his famous paper. It is the only nonlinear component in these schemes, and its strength is determined by it. As a result, building secure cryptographic protocols requires consideration about how to build a cryptography strong S-box. Over the last decade, academics from all around the globe have published a lot of studies on S-box. The substitution, however, is similar in each of these systems (or fixed). Elements changing permutation is studied in this thesis by thoroughly analyzing the cryptographic strengthening of the fundamental substitution operation. The dynamic S-box, which is similar to the dynamic look-up table suggested in, is a type of dynamic translation table.

The multiplicative inverse for a given number in Rijndael's finite field is used to generate the AES S-box. The affine transformation is then used to change the multiplicative inverse. A novel 6-dimensional DCMS with the Generalized Chaos Synchronization (GCS) property is proposed in the Generalized Chaos Synchronization (GCS) theorem. It is simple and convenient to generate a class of "good" S-box by adjusting the initial or system parameter significantly, thanks to the ideal features for sensitive dependant on initial condition and system parameter of the chaotic system. The affine transformation is added to fortify the S-box against algebraic attacks. There are three steps to the method: After generating an 8-bit series of binary random variables from a real value trajectory and converting it to a decimal integer via iterating a chaotic map, an integer table may be obtained. Second, a permuted integer sequence can be obtained by iterating the DCMS with the beginning value. Finally, the sequence is translated to a table, but each table entry is modified using the affine transformation, producing the S-box we require.

5.9 TANNER SCHEMATIC S-BOX DESIGN

S-Box with HERL logic is designed and simulated using Tanner EDA with 65nm technology. The efficiency of the proposed HERL XOR and S-Box are analyzed in terms of area, power consumption, delay, and energy consumption. Energy-efficient 8-bit S-Box is designed for cryptography applications. It is designed using HERL logic which is vulnerable to DPA and this logic is obtained by merging ECRL logic and PFAL logic. The proposed HERL XOR gate is designed and simulated using Tanner EDA with 125 nm technology. The proposed HERL XOR gate reduces the power consumption by 7.75%, 21.12%, 15.51%, 8.18%, 7.67% and 3.87% when compared with existing adiabatic logic techniques such as ECRL, PFAL, DCB PFAL, Modified SQAL, 2N-2N2P and IDPAL. The proposed S-Box design with HERL logic reduces the energy consumption by 35.14%, 42.17%, 30.67% and 10.46% when compared with the previous techniques such as ECRL, PFAL, DCB PFAL, 2N-2N2P and IDPAL. The Tanner schematic diagram of S-Box design using the proposed HERL XOR gate is shown in Figure 5.2.

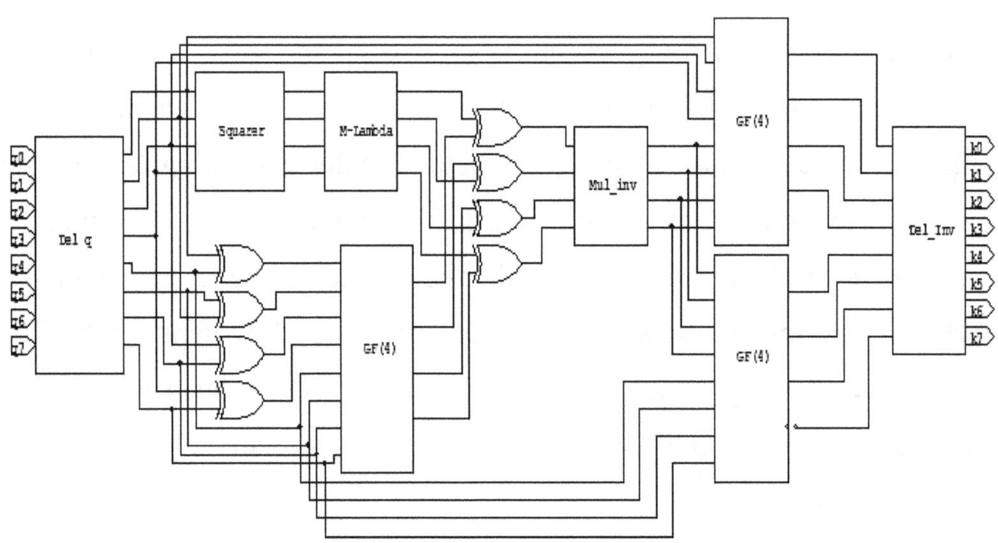

Figure 5.2 Tanner Schematic Diagram of S-Box design with proposed HERL XOR

5.10 POWER ANALYSIS OF S-BOX

Power consumption and energy consumption of various adiabatic logic techniques are compared and tabulated in Table 5.2.

Table 5.2 Power analysis of S-Box design

Technique	Average power (uW)	Energy Consumption (pJ)
ECRL	367.22	18452.80
PFAL	363.06	19412.81
DCB PFAL	360.59	17841.99
2N-2N2P	362.78	15882.50
IDPAL	355.23	14454.30
HERL	351.72	13653.77

From the tabulated results, it is observed that the proposed S-Box design with HERL logic reduces the energy consumption by 35.14%, 42.17%, 30.67% and 10.46% when compared with the previous techniques such as ECRL, PFAL, DCB PFAL, 2N-2N2P and IDPAL.

5.11 DELAY ANALYSIS OF S-BOX

The delay of S-Box design with various adiabatic logic techniques is compared and it is depicted in Figure 5.3.

From the comparison chart, it is cleared that the proposed S-Box design reduces the delay by 29.44%, 37.73%, 27.46%, 12.77% and 4.81% when compared with ECRL, PFAL, DCB PFAL, 2N-2N2P and IDPAL.

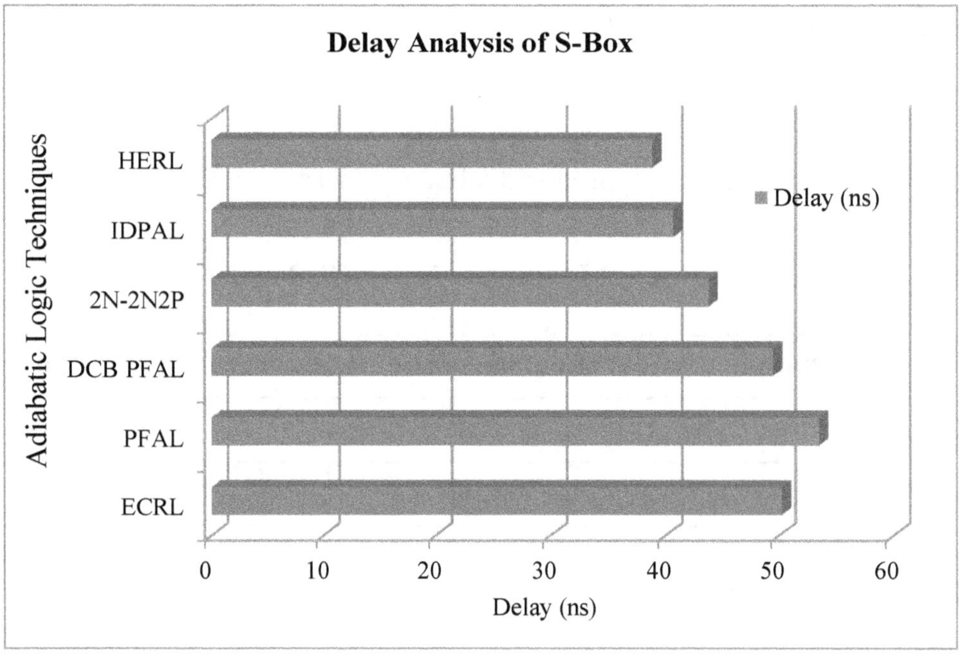

Figure 5.3 Delay Analysis of S-Box

5.12 TRANSISTOR COUNT AND POWER CONSUMPTION OF S-BOX DESIGN

Transistor count of S-Box design using various adiabatic logic techniques are tabulated in Table 5.3.

Table 5.3 Transistor count of S-Box design

Technique	Transistor count
ECRL	1804
PFAL	2320
DCB PFAL	2159
2N-2N2P	2020
IDPAL	2304
HERL	1804

Area of S-Box design with various adiabatic logic techniques are analyzed in terms of transistors. From the tabulated results, it is observed that the proposed S-Box with HERL reduces the number of transistors by 28.60%, 19.67%, 11.97% and 27.71% over other existing techniques such as S-Box with PFAL, DCB PFAL, 2N-2N2P and IDPAL. The number of transistors in the proposed S-Box with HERL is same as S-Box with ECRL. But the proposed HERL is efficient in terms of speed and power consumption when compared with ECRL.

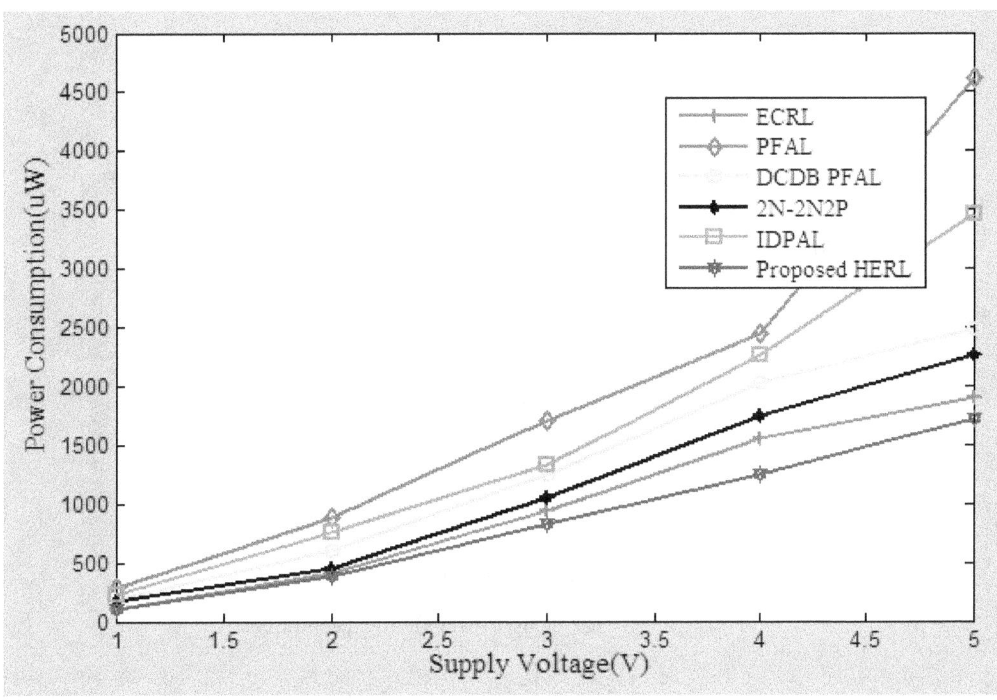

Figure 5.4 Power consumption Vs Supply Voltage of S-Box design

The power consumption of S-Box architecture with different adiabatic logic techniques are computed by varying the supply from 1V to 5V. From the above comparison graph, it is observed that the power consumption of the proposed HERL based S-Box design is lesser than existing S-Box designs.

5.13 PERFORMANCE EVALUATION OF PROPOSED S-BOX DESIGN

In Figure 5.5, the area of a GHERL XOR based S-Box design is computed based on the transistor count and compared to other S-Box designs. When compared to S-Box with sleep transistor, S-Box with dual sleep, S-Box with dual-stack, and S-Box with sleepy keeper approach, the proposed S-Box design with GHERL XOR gate reduces the number of transistors by 12.17 percent, 24.34 percent, 36.51 percent, and 12.17 percent, respectively.

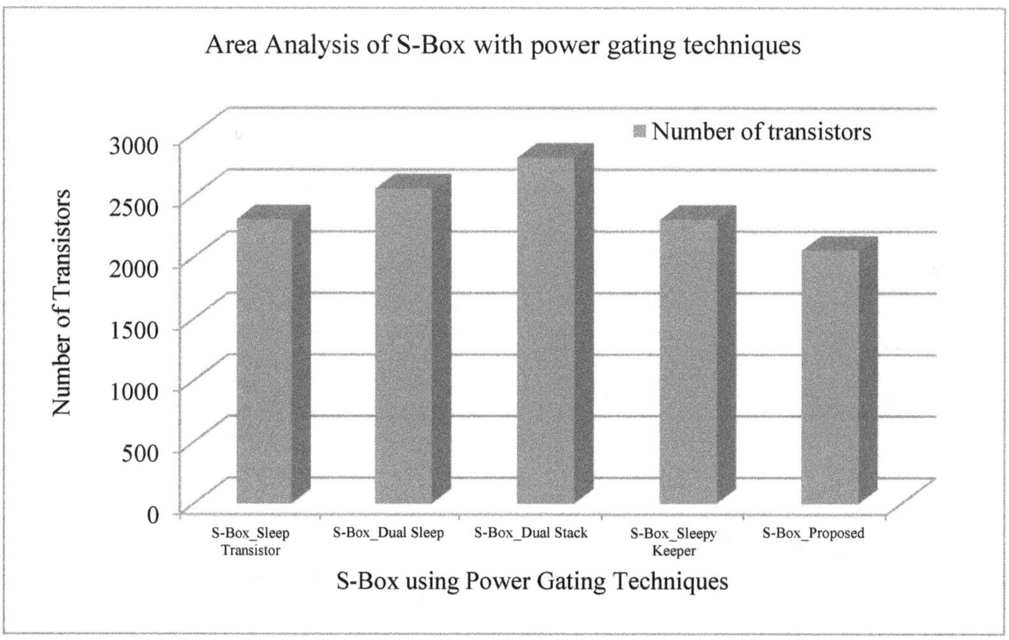

Figure 5.5 Area Analysis of S-Box with various power gating techniques

Table 5.4 shows the time taken by the S-Box design to finish the procedure and the energy spent by the S-Box design using power gating approaches. The energy consumption is measured in femto joules (1 femto = 10-15) and the delay is measured in nanoseconds. S-Box with sleep transistor power gating has the same latency as the proposed S-Box.

Table 5.4 Delay and energy consumption of S-Box with power gating techniques

Technique	Delay (ns)	Energy Consumption (fJ)
S-Box with Sleep Transistor	1.009	1.831
S-Box with Dual Sleep	1.003	2.763
S-Box with Dual Stack	2.68	7.564
S-Box with Sleepy Approach	2.01	6.078
S-Box with GHERL XOR	1.009	1.799

Table 5.4 shows that when compared to S-Box designs using dual sleep transistor power gating technique, the novel S-Box design reduces speed by 0.59 percent and increases speed by 62.35 percent and 49.80 percent, respectively, when compared to S-Box designs using dual-stack and sleepy keeper approaches. The secret key is retrieved by adversaries in most security applications through information leakage, which is usually in the form of power consumption. As a result, it is necessary to demonstrate the suggested S-Box design's efficiency in terms of power usage. In cryptography applications, a reduction in leakage information as a result of power dissipation leads to high security, implying that power dissipation is inversely proportional to security. The amount of power consumed by different power gating strategies is compared and presented in Figure 5.6.

When compared to current strategies such as S-Box with sleep transistor, dual sleep transistor, dual-stack, and sleepy keeper approach, Figure 5.6 indicates that the innovative S-Box design with GHERL XOR reduces power consumption by 1.76 percent, 35.26 percent, 36.81 percent, and 41.01 percent.

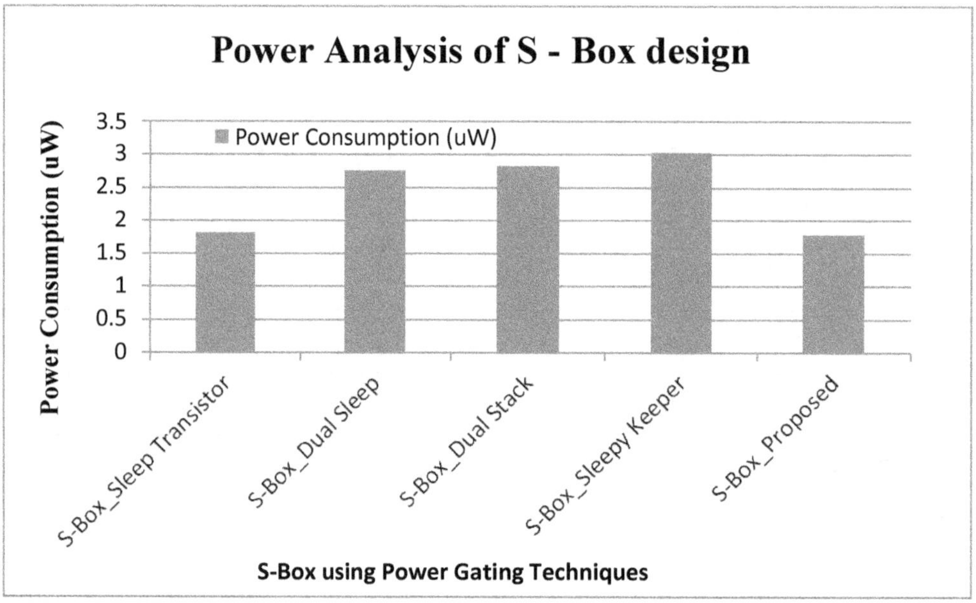

Figure 5.6 Power consumption of S-Box with various power gating techniques

5.14 SUMMARY

When security is the major concern in the modern digital world; Cryptographic systems are used in all portable and mobile devices applications. Cryptographic systems have high power consumption because of its complex architecture. Because of these reasons it is vulnerable to DPA attacks and also affects the battery lifespan. To address these issues many adiabatic logic techniques were used in the design of Cryptographic systems that are discussed in the literature. This proposed adiabatic logic styles HERL and GHERL are the most energy efficient circuit design method compared with other adiabatic techniques.

The S-Box design, which is ideal for high security applications, was the focus of this research. This study presented two different XOR gates, dubbed HERL XOR and GHERL XOR, to do this. ECRL and PFAL are two alternative adiabatic logic techniques used to create HERL XOR.

HERL logic and power gating are used to create the GHERL XOR gate. HERL XOR is primarily used for creating a space-saving S-Box design. The GHERL XOR gate is intended for use in the creation of an energy-efficient S-Box architecture. Because the suggested GHERL XOR used power gating, the leakage information was decreased by lowering the leakage power. As a result, the suggested S-Box design can achieve high energy efficiency while also providing excellent security.

The research effort can be expanded in the future to build an inverted S-Box design, which is essential for the decryption process. Furthermore, power gating and adiabatic logic techniques will be adjusted to provide S-Box architecture with fewer transistors, higher security, and lower energy usage.

A CERTAIN INVESTIGATION ON S-BOX DESIGN WITH HYBRID ENERGY RECOVERY LOGIC FOR IOT APPLICATIONS

A THESIS

Submitted by

RUBAN GLADWIN M

in partial fulfillment of the requirements for the degree of

DOCTOR OF PHILOSOPHY

FACULTY OF INFORMATION AND COMMUNICATION ENGINEERING

ANNA UNIVERSITY

CHENNAI 600 025

JANUARY 2023

CHAPTER 6

CONCLUSION AND SCOPE FOR FUTURE WORK

This chapter contains a summary of the thesis's concluding remarks, as well as the thesis' contributions. There is also a need for more research in the area of Robust and Secure S-Box Design with Gated Hybrid Energy Recovery Logic (GHERL) for IoT Applications. The findings of a study involving Gated Hybrid Energy Recovery Logic (GHERL) have been reported. The results show that the novel S-Box design with GHERL XOR reduces power consumption by 1.76 percent, 35.26 percent, 36.81 percent, 41.01 percent, and reduces leakage power by 58.54 percent, 20.27 percent, 27.38 percent, 13.63 percent when compared to existing techniques such as S-Box with sleep transistor, dual sleep transistor, dual-stack, and sleepy keeper approach. The literature has given greater attention to ways for processing Gated Hybrid Energy Recovery Logic (GHERL). The final chapter will include the following goals:

i. To list out the major remark of the thesis.

ii. To suggest possible extensions for future work in the area of research.

6.1 CONCLUDING REMARKS

Due to the general rapid advancement of technology, portable electronic gadgets must have low power consumption and dissipation. Designers use numerous power dissipation approaches at multiple levels, such as abstraction, architectural level, system level, and so on, to make the design suitable for real-time applications. In this research, adiabatic logic is used to minimize power consumption by recycling the energy stored in the load capacitor at each clock cycle. The power gating strategy is used to reduce power usage. S-Box uses both of these strategies to achieve excellent security with minimal power dissipation and good energy efficiency.

Develop an area-efficient Hybrid Energy Recovery Logic (HERL) based XOR gate by integrating two separate adiabatic logic approaches, such as ECRL and PFAL, with an energy-efficient XOR gate using this research. By merging HERL and power gating techniques, a Gated Hybrid Energy Recovery Logic (GHERL) based XOR gate is constructed. S-Boxes were also designed utilizing HERL-based XOR gates and GHERL-based XOR gates to achieve low power, low area, fast speed, and low energy consumption.

Efficient Charge Recovery Logic (ECRL) and Positive Feedback Adiabatic Logic are two adiabatic logic approaches that are combined in Hybrid Energy Recovery Logic (HERL) (PFAL). It is appropriate for the S-Box design, which may be used in security applications. The Internet of Things (IoT) is a network that connects smart devices that require high security, energy efficiency, and low power consumption. Due to information loss, traditional AES is not suitable for high-security applications. To address this problem, AES employs the GHERL XOR gate, which combines adiabatic logic with power gating. Both are power-saving approaches that employ recovery logic to cut power usage and switch off current flow to inactive blocks.

This research concentrates on the S-Box design, which is suited for high-security applications. To do this, the researchers proposed two new XOR gates, termed HERL XOR and GHERL XOR. HERL XOR is made using two different adiabatic logic techniques: ECRL and PFAL. The GHERL XOR gate is made using HERL logic and power gating. The HERL XOR is primarily utilized to create a compact S-Box design. The GHERL XOR gate is designed to be used in an energy-efficient S-Box architecture. The leakage information was reduced by decreasing the leakage power because the recommended GHERL XOR employed power gating. As a consequence, the proposed S-Box design can both save energy and provide good security.

When compared to Diode Connected DC Biased PFAL (DCDB-PFAL), Modified Secured Quasi Adiabatic Logic (M-SQAL), and 2N-2N2P logic, the suggested HERL XOR gate lowers the area by 41.66 percent, 8.33 percent, and 16.66 percent, respectively. When compared to ECRL, PFAL, DCDB-PFAL, 2N-2N2P, and Input Decoupled Partially Adiabatic Logic, the suggested S-Box architecture with HERL XOR reduces power consumption by 4.41 percent, 3.22 percent, 2.52 percent, 3.14 percent, and 1.01 percent (IDPAL). When compared to the HERL XOR with sleep, dual sleep, dual-stack, and sleepy keeper approaches, the suggested GHERL XOR gate reduces power and energy consumption by 74.24 percent, 63.41 percent, 44.91 percent, 13.04 percent, and 87.34 percent, 26.60 percent, 3.61 percent, 13.97 percent.

6.2 SCOPE FOR FUTURE WORK

The following are some possibilities for further study in this area:

- • A more in-depth exploration of lightweight algorithms in order to promote their use in real-time.

- Development of security protocols based on lightweight cryptographic primitives in order to ensure the overall security of smart systems.
- S-box architectural design based on particular needs, implementation options, and optimization processes and algorithms.
- In the future, the research work might be broadened to create an inverted S-Box design, which is required for decryption.
- Power gating and adiabatic logic approaches will be tweaked to provide the S-Box design fewer transistors, stronger security, and reduced energy consumption.

REFERENCES

1. Aarushi Mann, Naman Malhotra, Abhishek Wadhwa & Neeta Pandey 2020, 'Power Gated ECRL Adiabatic Logic Based Optimized Two-Input Multiplexer', 17th India Council International Conference (INDICON), IEEE Conference Paper.

2. Adonis Bogris, Panagiotis Rizomiliotis, Konstantinos E Chlouverakis, Apostolos Argyris & Dimitris Syvridis 2008, 'Feedback Phase in Optically Generated Chaos: A Secret Key for Cryptographic Applications', IEEE Journal of Quantum Electronics vol. 44, issue 2 IEEE Journal Article.

3. Akash Agrawal, Tarun Kumar Gupta, Ajay Kumar Dadoria & Deepak Kumar 2016, 'A Novel Efficient Adiabatic Logic Design for Ultra Low Power', International Conference on ICT in Business Industry & Government (ICTBIG), IEEE Conference Paper.

4. Alejandro Freyre-Echevarría, Ismel Martínez-Díaz, Carlos Miguel Legón Pérez, Guillermo Sosa-Gómez & Omar Rojas 2020, 'Evolving Nonlinear S-Boxes With Improved Theoretical Resilience to Power Attacks", IEEE Access, vol. 8 IEEE Journal Article.

5. Arash Reyhani-Masoleh, Mostafa Taha & Doaa Ashmawy 2020, 'New Low-Area Designs for the AES Forward, Inverse and Combined S-boxes', IEEE Transactions on Computers, vol. 69, issue 12, IEEE Journal Article.

6. Ashwak Alabaichi & Adnan Ibrahem Salih 2015, 'Enhance security of advance encryption standard algorithm based on key-dependent S box', 2015 fifth international conference on digital information processing and communications (icdipc), ieee conference paper.

7. Blotti S Borghese & Saletti, R 2002, 'Single-Inductor Four-Phase Power-Clock Generator For Positive-Feedback Adiabatic Logic Gates', 9th International Conference on Electronics, Circuits and Systems, vol. 2, IEEE Conference Paper.

8. Ch. Shravan, Ch. Pavan Kumar & Sivani, K 2014, 'A Novel Approach for Power-Gating Technique with Improved Efficient Charge

Recovery Logic', International Conference on Smart Electric Grid (ISEG), IEEE Conference Paper.

9. Christopher A Wood, Stanislaw P Radziszowski & Marcin Lukowiak 2015, 'Constructing Large S-boxes with Area Minimized Implementations', MILCOM IEEE Military Communications Conference, IEEE Conference Paper.

10. Daheng Yue, Yan Sun, Minxuan Zhang, Shaoqing Li & Yutong Dai 2009, 'A Look-Up Table Based Differential Logic to counteract DPA attacks', 8th International Conference on ASIC, IEEE Conference Paper, p. 1.

11. Dao-Shun Wang, Tao Song, Lin Dong & Ching-Nung Yang 2013, 'Optimal Contrast Grayscale Visual Cryptography Schemes with Reversing', IEEE Transactions on Information Forensics and Security, vol. 8, issue 12, IEEE Journal Article.

12. David J Willingham & Izzet Kale 2008, 'Using Positive Feedback Adiabatic Logic to implement Reversible Toffoli Gates', Norchip, IEEE Conference Paper.

13. Dinesh Kumar, S, Himanshu Thapliyal & Azhar Mohammad 2018, 'FinSAL: FinFET based Secure Adiabatic Logic for Energy-Efficient and DPA Resistant IoT Devices', IEEE Transactions on Computer-Aided Design of Integrated Circuits and Systems, vol. 37, issue 1.

14. Elana Andrews, P & Dhanesh, MS 2017, 'A body biased adiabatic dynamic differential logic(BADDL) to prevent DPA attacks in smart cards', International Conference on Intelligent Computing and Control Systems (ICICCS), IEEE Conference Paper, Cited by: Papers vol. 3.

15. Ganesh Khedkar, Dhireesha Kudithipudi & Garrett S Rose 2015, 'Power Profile Obfuscation Using Nanoscale Memristive Devices to Counter DPA Attacks', IEEE Transactions on nanotechnology, vol. 14, issue 1, Journal Article, IEEE Access, p.11.

16. Jia Wang, Lee-Ming Cheng & Tong Su 2018, 'Multivariate cryptography based on clipped Hopfield neural Network', IEEE transactions on neural networks and learning systems, vol. 29, issue 2, Journal Article.

17. Julia Juremi, Ramlan Mahmod & Salasiah Sulaiman 2012, 'A Proposal for Improving AES S-box with Rotation and Key-Dependent', Proceedings Title: 2012 International Conference on Cyber Security, Cyber Warfare and Digital Forensic (CyberSec), IEEE Conference Paper.

18. Kaedi, S, Doostari, MA & Ghaznavi-Ghoushchi, MB 2019, 'A DPA Attack on IOA Data-Dependent Delay Counter measure Based on an Inherent Tempo-Spatial Data Dependency', IEEE Transactions on Circuits and Systems II: Express Briefs, vol. 66, issue 8, Journal Article, IEEE.

19. Kaedi, V, Doostari, MA & Ghaznavi-Ghoushchi, MB 2019, 'A DPA Attack on IOA Data-Dependent Delay Countermeasure Based on an Inherent Tempo-Spatial Data Dependency', IEEE Journal Article, IEEE Transactions on Circuits and Systems II: Express Briefs vol. 66, issue 8.

20. Kavi Priya, S & Arunmani, G 2019, 'Advanced Logic Level Design Methodology for a Secure DPA Resistant FPGA', 2019 IEEE International Conference on Intelligent Techniques in Control, Optimization and Signal Processing (INCOS), Conference Paper, IEEE Access, p.2.

21. Kazuyuki Tanimura & Nikil D Dutt 2012, 'HDRL: Homogeneous Dual Rail Logic for DPA Attack Resistive Secure Circuit Design', IEEE Access, vol. 4, issue 3, p. 7.

22. Kazuyuki Tanimura & Nikil Dutt 2010,'ExCCel: Exploration of complementary cells for efficient DPA attack resistivity', IEEE International Symposium on Hardware-Oriented Security and Trust (HOST), IEEE Conference Paper, p. 3.

23. Keote, ML &Karule, PT 2015, 'Design and Implementation of Energy Efficient Adiabatic ECRL and Basic Gates', International Conference on Soft Computing Techniques and Implementations (ICSCTI), IEEE Conference Paper.

24. Kimmo Jarvinen & Jorma Skytta 2008, 'On Parallelization of High-Speed Processors for Elliptic Curve Cryptography', IEEE Transactions on Very Large Scale Integration (VLSI) Systems vol. 16, issue 9, IEEE Journal Article.

25. Martin Petrvalsky, Milos Drutarovsky & Michal Varchola 2016, 'Compact MCU-based platform for a side channel resistant firmware development and evaluation – a case study for an DPA attack on a multi precision multiplication', 26th International Conference Radioelektronika (Radioelektronika), IEEE Conference Paper.

26. Miao Yuan & Guoqiang Bai 2015, 'Improving Second Order DPA Attacks with New Modeled Power Leakages', 11th International Conference on Computational Intelligence and Security (CIS), IEEE Conference Paper.

27. Moshe Avital, Hadar Dagan, Itamar Levi, Osnat Keren & Alexander Fish 2015, 'DPA-Secured Quasi-Adiabatic Logic (SQAL) for Low-Power Passive RFID Tags Employing S-Boxes', IEEE Transactions on Circuits and Systems I: Regular Papers vol. 62, issue 1, IEEE Journal Article.

28. Muhtahir O Oloyede & Gerhard P Hancke 2016, 'Unimodal and Multimodal Biometric Sensing Systems: A Review', vol. 4, IEEE Access, Journal Article.

29. Musheer Ahmad, Eesa Al-Solami, Ahmed Mohammed Alghamdi & Muhammad Awais Yousaf 2020, 'Bijective S-Boxes Method Using Improved Chaotic Map-Based Heuristic Search and Algebraic Group Structures', IEEE Access, vol. 8, IEEE Journal Article.

30. Nabihah Ahmad, Rezaul Hasan; Warsuzarina & Mat Jubadi 2010, 'Design of AES S-Box using combinational logic Optimization', IEEE Symposium on Industrial Electronics and Applications (ISIEA),Conference Paper.

31. Po-Chun Liu, Hsie-Chia Chang & Chen-Yi Lee 2010, 'A Low Overhead DPA Countermeasure Circuit Based on Ring Oscillators', IEEE Transactions on circuits and Systems II: Express Briefs vol. 57, issue 7.

32. Rahaman, H, Mathew, J & Pradhan, DK 2010, 'Secure Testable S-box Architecture for Cryptographic Hardware Implementation', OUP Journal Article The Computer Journal vol. 53, issue 5.

33. Ratanpal, GB, Williams, RD & Blalock, TN 2004, 'An on chip signal suppression countermeasure to power analysis attacks', IEEE Transactions on Dependable and Secure Computing, IEEE Access, vol.1, issue 3, p.75.

34. Saleh Ibrahim & Alaa M Abbas 2020,'"A Novel Optimization Method for Constructing Cryptographically Strong Dynamic S-Boxes', IEEE Access, vol. 8, p.6.

35. Satyanarayana Vollala, VV Varadhan, K. Geetha, N & Ramasubramanian 2014, 'Efficient Modular Multiplication Algorithms for Public Key Cryptography', International Advance Computing Conference (IACC), IEEE Conference Paper.

36. Shiny, RM, Jayalakshmi, P, Rajakrishnammal, A, Sivaprabha, T & Abirami, R 2016, 'An Efficient Tagged Visual Cryptography for Color Images', International Conference on Computational Intelligence and Computing Research (ICCIC), IEEE Conference Paper.

37. Shiv Pratap, Singh Kushawaha & Trailokya Nath Sasamal 2015, 'Modified Positive Feedback Adiabatic Logic for Ultra Low Power VLSI', International Conference on Computer, Communication and Control (IC4), IEEE Conference Paper.

38. Sonal Aron, Shelly Garg & Vandana Niranjan 2015, 'PFAL Based Power Efficient Mux Based Decoder', International Conference on Computing, Communication & Automation, IEEE Conference Paper.

39. Subhashini, R & Geetha, M 2014, 'Efficient Charge Recovery Logic for Power Gating in Logic Circuits', International Conference on Green Computing Communication and Electrical Engineering (ICGCCEE), IEEE Conference Paper.

40. Walid El-Shafai, Iman M Almomani & Aala Alkhayer 2021, 'Optical Bit-Plane Based 3D-JST Cryptography Algorithm With Cascaded 2D-FrFT Encryption for Efficient and Secure HEVC Communication', vol. 9 IEEE Access, IEEE Journal Article.

41. Wei Liu, Liji Wu, Xiangmin Zhang & An Wang 2014, 'Wavelet-Based Noise Reduction in Power Analysis Attack', Tenth International Conference on Computational Intelligence and Security, IEEE Conference Paper, p. 10.

42. Weijia Wang, Yu Yu, François-Xavier Standaert, Junrong Liu, Zheng Guo & Dawu Gu 2018, 'Ridge Based DPA: Improvement of Differential Power Analysis For Nano scale Chips', vol. 13, p. 19, Issue: 5IEEE Transactions on Information Forensics and Security.

43. Weize Yu & Selçuk Köse 2016, 'A Voltage Regulator Assisted Light weight AES Implementation against DPA Attacks', IEEE Transactions on Circuits and Systems, IEEE Access, vol. 63, issue 8, p.37.

44. Willliam Morell & Ashok Srivastava 2018, 'Evaluation of Four Power Gating Schemes Applied to ECRL Adiabatic Logic', 61st International Midwest Symposium on Circuits and Systems (MWSCAS), IEEE Conference Paper.

45. Xiang Wang, Qingqi Pei & Hui Li 2014, 'A Lossless Tagged Visual Cryptography Scheme', IEEE Signal Processing Letters, vol. 21, issue 7, IEEE Journal Article.

46. Xiangdong Yin 2010, 'S Box Construction and Result Analysis Based on Optimal Tabu genetic Algorithm', 2nd International Conference on Education Technology and Computer, vol. 3, IEEE Conference Paper.

47. Xuefei Bai, Li Guo, Lu Huang &Yanhua Xu 2009, 'A Fast VLSI Design of SMS4 Cipher Based on Twisted BDD S-Box Architecture', International Conference on Networks Security, Wireless Communications and Trusted Computing IEEE Conference Paper vol. 1.

48. Yiqun Zhang, Li Xu, Qing Dong, Jingcheng Wang, David Blaauw & Dennis Sylvester 2018, 'Recryptor: A Reconfigurable Cryptographic Cortex-M0 Processor with In-Memory and Near-Memory Computing for IoT Security', IEEE Journal of Solid-State Circuits, vol. 53,issue 4, IEEE Journal Article, 2018.

49. Yu Sasaki & Yosuke Todo 2018, 'Tight Bounds of Differentially and Linearly Active S-boxes and Division Property of Lilliput', IEEE Transactions on Computers, vol. 67, issue 5 Journal Article.

50. Yuyu Zhang, Guoxi Wang, Yufeng Ma & Jingwen Li 2011, 'A Comprehensive Design Method Based on WDDL and Dynamic Cryptosystem to Resist DPA Attack', 2011 International Conference on Intelligence Science and Information Engineering, IEEE Conference Paper.

51. Zeeshan Kaleem & Kyunghi Chang 2016, 'Public Safety Priority-Based User Association for Load Balancing and Interference Reduction in PS-LTE Systems', IEEE Access vol. 4 IEEE Journal Article.

52. Zhenfei Zhang, Willy Susilo & Raad Raad 2008, 'Mobile Ad-hoc Network Key Management with Certificateless Cryptography', 2nd International Conference on Signal Processing and Communication Systems, IEEE Conference Paper.

53. Yong Moon and Deog-Kyoon Jeong, "An efficient charge recovery logic circuit," in IEEE Journal of Solid-State Circuits, vol. 31, no. 4, pp. 514-522, April 1996, doi: 10.1109/4.499727.

54. Neil H.E. Weste, David Money Harris —CMOS VLSI Design: A Circuits and Systems Perspective‖, 4th Edition, Pearson , 2017.

LIST OF PUBLICATIONS

International Journal

1. **Ruban Gladwin, M** & Kasthuri, N 2022, 'Robust and Secure S-Box Design with Gated Hybrid Energy Recovery Logic (GHERL) for IOT Applications', *DYNA*, January, vol. 97, no. 1, p.79-84. ISSN 0012-7361, **Impact Factor: 1.334**.

www.ingramcontent.com/pod-product-compliance
Lightning Source LLC
LaVergne TN
LVHW082350200926
848481LV00012B/3520